DROP SHIPPING
For
SELLERS

Lloyd J Boone

Drop Shipping For Sellers

Lloyd J Boone

Published by Lulu:

http://www.lulu.com

All rights reserved. No part of this book may be reproduced or transmitted in any form, or by any means, electronic or mechanical, including screen capture, scanning, recording, photocopying, or by any information storage and retrieval system, without express written permission from the author, except for the inclusion of brief quotations in a review.

Copyright © 2007 by Lloyd J Boone.

ISBN (13): 978-1-4303-1109-6
ISBN (10): 1-4303-1109-6

About The Author

Lloyd J Boone is a businessman residing in Toronto, Canada. He holds a Bachelor Degree in Business from York University, a MBA Certificate in Accounting from Heriot-Watt University, along with a number of other credentials from such institutions as Ryerson University and OCAD. In addition, he has completed a number of courses and seminars from such recognized experts as Tom Peters, Tony Robbins, Dan Poynter and others.

Lloyd's extensive business background spans almost three decades, including more than a decade of Internet marketing experience during which time he introduced such products to the marketplace as the Exploit Submission Wizard, FFA Blaster and EnginePoster Website Submission Software. He authored a number of books and articles on Internet Marketing, including a marketing newsletter (Marcap Communicator) to an opt-in subscription base of more than 145,000 members, plus an online NAFTA Trade Directory showcasing a wide variety of companies in various sectors of the North American economy.

Before becoming involved in the various aspects of the Internet, Lloyd spent a number of years in Financial Consulting following a 6-year term as Director of Finance for Call-Net Telecommunications, prior to its Sprint Canada branding agreement in 1993. Prior to Call-Net, Lloyd spent a number of years in finance at various companies including a local CA Firm.

Lloyd has been dealing with eBay since 2001, and with PayPal since 2000, as well as with a number of other marketing/auction sites such as Amazon and Yahoo, and with other payment processing facilities such as ClickBank, iBill and

BidPay, involving a total of more than 100,000 transactions both as a merchant, and as a customer.

Lloyd has also developed extensive skills in Art and Photography, acquired from both his experience, and from his formal education at Ryerson and OCAD. His work has been featured at a couple of local art galleries, and he was twice media/photo credentialed for the Molson Indy, first in 2003, and then again in 2005.

Disclaimer

The reader acknowledges that while every effort has been made to verify the accuracy and completeness of the information contained within this book, errors and omissions may still occur.

The content of this book should therefore be used only as a starting point from which to build a possible wholesaler/retailer relationship, and only then, after the reader has performed his own due diligence on the information provided. The information in this book should not be used, or relied upon, for any other purpose.

As with any business venture, it should be understood that there are always certain risks involved. It is the responsibility of the participants to investigate any claims made with respect to products or services offered, so as to determine the degree of such risks.

It should be further understood that neither the author nor the publisher makes any claims, warranties or representations as to the inclusiveness or completeness of any of the information provided herein. Nor does the author or the publisher in any way vouch for the integrity of any of the sources listed.

Finally, the information contained within this book is not in any way intended to be, nor to replace, standard legal advice. Any legal advice required should be obtained through the services of a competent attorney experienced in such a field. Any recommendations made are presented solely as an opinion of the author, which have been found to be most effective in the author's ongoing course of doing business.

Acknowledgements

The Author would like to offer a special thanks to both eBay and PayPal for their input, both direct and indirect, into the authoring of this book.

The Author acknowledges that while there are certain recommendations and procedures presented herein for dealing with various situations which may arise, they are not in any way intended to replace any *official* rules regarding the same, nor to circumvent any law which might exist to the contrary. For greater certainty, should there be any conflict between what the author has suggested, and what any official rule or law may require, the official rule or law should always apply.

The Author would like to thank Nikon for providing information on its warranty policy, and for the use of that information within this book.

The Author would like to offer a very special thank-you to Dan Poynter, of Para Publishing, for his excellent help and support in getting this project off the ground.

Cover Clipart for this book has been provided under license agreement with iClipart.com.

Cover Design and Layout by Lloyd J Boone.

And last, but certainly not least, the Author would like to offer a very special thanks to Sylvia Hoekstra, whose work in both research and proof-reading contributed so greatly to this book, and without whose personal support, this book would likely not have been written.

Table of Contents

About The Author	3
Disclaimer	5
Acknowledgements	7
Chapter 1: An Overview	**11**
Greetings & Thank You!	11
What To Expect From This Book	11
Drop Shipping's New Paradigm	12
Competition: The Big Bad Wolf	13
More Than Just Price	13
The Seller's Reputation	14
Buyer Fraud	15
Buyer Scrutiny	17
Payment Methods Accepted	17
Stocking Best Sellers	18
False Claims Of List Providers	19
Drop Ship Catalog & Website Scams	20
False Testimonials	22
Chapter 2: Drop Shipping Basics	**25**
What Is Drop Shipping?	25
Drop Shipper Lists & Their Providers	26
The Pros & Cons Of Drop Shipping	32
Chapter 3: Selecting A Drop Shipper	**37**
Checking Status Of Drop Shipper	37
Physical Location Of Drop Shipper	40
Building A Partnership	41
Drop Shipper's Terms & Conditions	41

Chapter 4: Choosing, Pricing & Listing Items   **51**
    Choosing Products   51
    Setting Prices   54
    Listing Items   57

Chapter 5: Payment Methods   **73**
    Are You Losing Business?   73
    Merchant Accounts & Credit Card Services   74
    PayPal   77
    Other Payment Processing Services   80
    Protection For Sellers   80
    Fraud Prevention   82

Chapter 6: Identity Theft   **85**
    Phishing & Spoof E-Mail   85
    Reading E-Mail Headers   87
    Account Hi-Jacking   90
    Heed The Warnings   94

Chapter 7: Dealing With Customers   **95**
    The Customer Is Always Right   95
    Item & Delivery Disputes   96
    Leaving Feedback For Your Buyers   98
    Non-Paying Bidders   100
    Mutual Feedback Withdrawal   101
    The Responsibility Rests With You   102

Afterword   **105**

Glossary   **107**

Special Offer   **115**

Chapter 1

An Overview

Greetings & Thank You!

Perhaps you are new to the concept of *Drop Shipping*. Or, maybe you are quite experienced in that area of retailing, and are now looking for additional sources through which to complement your current product line. Many of you may already have your own websites from which you offer various products for sale, while others of you may view eBay as your new business frontier. And of course, no doubt, there are some of you who already do, or plan to do, both.

Whatever your status, I would like to thank you for purchasing this book, and hope that you will find it most valuable.

What To Expect From This Book

This book will not only provide you with a very thorough *working* knowledge of *Drop Shipping*, but it should also give you a good insight into how both eBay and PayPal operate. And while much of this book does focus primarily on eBay as a marketing venue, and on PayPal as the preferred payment processing method, most of the tips and techniques covered can be easily applied to many different aspects of retailing, both online and off.

It is an extensive Drop Shipping "how to" guide, with the

odd "how not to" thrown in for good measure. In other words, it includes not only what you should always expect from any *Drop Shipping* service, and in doing business on eBay, but equally important, it includes what you should avoid. It is broken down into 7 Chapters...

- Chapter 1 (this Chapter) is an overview of this book.
- In Chapter 2, you will discover what *Drop Shipping* is, and even more importantly, you will discover precisely how the entire process should unfold, thus helping you to avoid many of the pitfalls which you might otherwise encounter.
- Chapter 3 will guide you through the various steps necessary in order to find and select compatible Wholesale Drop Shippers with which to build equitable and lasting relationships.
- In Chapter 4, you will learn not only how to choose actual products, but you will be provided with guidelines for setting their selling prices, as well as specifics in just how your items should, and should not be listed.
- Chapter 5 will cover the various payment processing options available to you, as well as provide you with an in-depth look at the pros and cons associated with each option.
- In Chapter 6, the focus will be on Identity Theft, including Phishing and Spoofing, with ways to spot it and avoid it.
- Chapter 7 will provide you with many tools and techniques to help you better deal with your customers, ensuring that your online marketing experience will be as happy and as profitable as possible.

Drop Shipping's New Paradigm

While *Drop Shipping* is certainly not by any means a new concept, its logistics can be considered somewhat new as they apply to eBay, or to similar closed-style marketing venues. In days gone by, it was not uncommon to see a magazine advertisement for an item, with a notation to allow as long as

6-8 weeks for delivery.

Today, such long delivery times are totally unacceptable. In fact, any seller who shows such poor performance today will not be around for long, not to mention that if he is an eBay seller, his reputation will be anything but acceptable. These days, delivery times of greater than 21 days will not sit well with buyers. And sellers who use *Drop Shipping* must perform within those same expected parameters, or they will receive far more negative feedback and non-delivery complaints than might otherwise be the case.

Competition: The Big Bad Wolf

As any business person knows, competition is in many ways, a very nasty word. All too often, it plays an all too significant role in virtually every aspect of any sales-based organization, not to mention providing more than a few headaches for those who run them. This is particularly true when selling on eBay.

Competition is something which must be given much more than just a cursory thought. Your ability to understand and work within its parameters is what will either make you or break you in the online retail business. Ignorance of that fact will ensure that you are not in business for very long, at least not on eBay. Make no mistake about it! Online retailers must have the innate ability to immediately adapt to their surroundings, especially when their competition is likely no more than a mere mouse-click away.

More Than Just Price

Often the first thing which comes to a retailer's mind when thinking of his competition, is price. This is why so many retailers offer price match guarantees, and the like. Such retailers believe that price is what will win and keep a customer. Unfortunately, sometimes to their complete detriment, they discover that they were wrong. Price was not the main concern their customers had, nor did having lower prices in any way command customer loyalty. That is the way it is in the 'bricks & mortar' world. That is the way it is in cyberspace. Dealing on eBay is no different.

As their counter-parts in the concrete world have discovered, so too have eBay sellers discovered, often the hard way, that price is not the # 1 consideration which experienced buyers have in determining which products to purchase, and the sellers from whom to purchase them. Perhaps even more so than in the 'bricks & mortar' world, the location of the seller plays a very major part. Buyers want to be reasonably assured that they will receive the products they order in a timely manner, and they need to know that they will not have to incur needless extra expenses, due to increased shipping costs, import duties and taxes over which neither they nor their sellers will have any control. But there is one other aspect which eBay sellers must consider that their 'bricks & mortar' or other online counter-parts normally do not have to. Sellers on eBay must consider their feedback reputations, because it is by such reputations that they are ultimately judged.

The Seller's Reputation

Buyers on eBay will more likely than not, consider closely the reputations of the sellers they hope to deal with. They are able to do this by reviewing the individual feedback profiles of their potential sellers. Buyers want to be able to determine from a seller's feedback whether or not that seller is reliable. They want to know that they will receive the products they order and pay for in a timely manner. And they want to know if those products will be exactly as described in the auctions they bid on. Over time, a seller's feedback profile should reflect this information quite accurately.

The ability to leave feedback for a seller after a transaction is completed, indeed gives eBay buyers a tremendous advantage which most other online buyers do not have. Imagine dealing directly with some unknown online merchant from his own website! Will you receive the item you pay for? Will it be as advertised? There would be no guarantee, and there would perhaps be no recourse if something were to go wrong. It should be no surprise why this is one of the prime reasons eBay has become so popular, and has experienced such rapid growth over the past few years, making it not only the largest, but quite arguably the most respected marketing venue in the world.

Is eBay seller feedback 100% accurate and reliable? Of course not! Few things in life are! Sadly, there are many games which both sellers and buyers play in order to manipulate their overall eBay feedback numbers. But still, even though the eBay feedback system may not be perfect, it is still vastly better than nothing at all. With experience, a shrewd person can learn to often read between the lines, and in many cases, read a lot more from what is not there, than from what is. Call that gut instinct if you will. I prefer to call it skill.

Of course you may think that you are the absolute best and most honest seller in the world, and you may very well be. But unless you maintain a sparkling feedback reputation, your overall sales will suffer greatly for it. There are some who claim that eBay feedback means very little. They claim that many buyers do not even bother reading an auction page, let alone a seller's feedback profile. That way of thinking is generally not accurate, and would indeed be a poor approach to selling on eBay.

There are of course some buyers, especially those new to eBay, who are not nearly as careful as they ought to be when it comes to reading an auction page description, or in viewing a seller's feedback profile. As a result, they sometimes end up purchasing something quite different from what they thought they were buying. Or in more extreme cases, they may even end up getting cheated by unethical sellers whose sole intention is to take advantage of such buyers. But those are the exceptions to the rule, rather than the norm.

Buyer Fraud

At the opposite end of the scale, are those buyers who do indeed read auction descriptions and seller profiles very closely. They are the informed consumers who are not likely to make careless mistakes, nor are they likely to be taken advantage of, as they fully understand what they are doing. Unfortunately, among this group are also a number of buyers who have anything but honorable intentions. Their evil plan is to determine exactly how their targeted sellers operate, such as whether they leave feedback immediately after payment is received, or whether they ship items with tracking information, etc. They then use that information to obtain products without ever having to pay for them. Those are the buyers who present the biggest problems for inexperienced sellers, who unfortunately do not yet fully understand what they need to do in order to protect themselves.

Scam buyers will purchase items, often with credit cards not belonging to them. Sometimes they will use their own credit cards, but with the sole intention of charging back amounts after they receive the items they purchased. This is very easy for them to do, since they have most likely already determined from either the S&H amount charged, or from the seller's feedback profile, whether or not their targeted seller can track items shipped.

eBay estimates that less than 1% of its auctions involve fraudulent activity. Even if we were to double or triple that estimate, I suspect that it would still be a far cry less than the number of incidents of fraud experienced from a similar number of online transactions conducted outside of eBay, where incidents of fraud are estimated to be as high as 1 in 4 (25%). Nonetheless, I believe that most fraud could be eliminated, whether it is taking place on or off eBay. All it takes is more awareness on the part of both buyers and sellers. It will however require people to take responsibility for their own actions, and not always try to shift the blame to someone else for their own shortcomings. But that is not the focus of *this* book.

While the actual number of cases of buyer fraud is somewhat low in the overall scheme of things, it is certainly something which all sellers should be very much aware of. This is especially important if selling higher priced items. The bottom line is that scam buyers know how to target less-informed sellers, just as scam sellers know how to target less-informed buyers.

The long and the short of it, is that if you ship items without tracking, you will not be able to prove delivery. As such, you will lose your money in virtually all cases that buyers claim non-delivery, as you will be unable to prove that the item was in fact delivered.

Buyer Scrutiny

In general, I believe that most buyers do indeed read auction descriptions as well as view seller feedback, and that they do so for only good intentions. In fact, many buyers will ask a question or two about an item before bidding on it. Some will even do so merely to test the responsiveness of a particular seller, rather than actually having some other reason to know the answer to the question being asked. If as a seller, you ignore such questions, even if the answers are already on your auction page, or you are rude in your replies, you will be throwing potential sales out the window.

As a result of this buyer scrutiny, often identical products sell for much more from sellers with excellent feedback, and quick polite responses to questions, than they do from sellers with lower feedback percentages, who rarely answer questions regarding the items they have listed. This is particularly true, and arguably much more important, when dealing with higher priced items, and with items where either warranty or authenticity are important factors.

Payment Methods Accepted

Other things which buyers consider very seriously are the payment methods which a seller accepts. If you as a seller, do not accept credit cards or PayPal, then you will likely not do well on eBay. Most buyers will avoid you like the plague, especially if your payment terms are restricted to only money orders or wire transfers. Such payment terms are more often than not, considered to be the MO (*modus operandi*) of scammers. In fact, more and more buyers have a tendency to avoid any auctions for which sellers do not accept PayPal as a method of payment. According to eBay, more than 90% of all eBay sellers now accept PayPal as a preferred method of payment for their auctions, while an ever growing number of sellers accept only PayPal as a method of payment.

This trend towards PayPal's universal acceptance is certainly evidenced by the recent rapid growth in its membership base, which now stands at over 100 million worldwide. If you are already familiar with PayPal, the reason for this rapid growth should be quite obvious. No other payment processing system offers both buyers and sellers alike the balanced level of transaction protection that PayPal does.

Any effective payment processing system should offer a good balance of protection for both buyers and sellers alike. It must not be one-sided. The level of protection offered should be such that as a legitimate seller, you can be reasonably assured of being paid for the items that you ship to your customers. You should not be victimized by unscrupulous buyers who make it their habit of purchasing items, and then charging back their credit cards after they receive their (your) items. At the same time, any fair and effective payment processing system should also provide an excellent level of protection to buyers who either do not receive the products they order and pay for, or else receive items substantially different from those advertised by sellers – sellers who sometimes lack a very high degree of integrity. PayPal provides such a balance. In fact, in my humble opinion, no other payment system on this planet offers such an excellent balance. As such, I would very strongly recommend PayPal to any merchant, whether selling on eBay or not, and especially so, if as a seller you intend to drop ship products to your customers. There will be much more on this later.

Stocking Best Sellers

While *Drop Shipping* is a fantastic way to sell numerous items without having to run many of the risks associated with purchasing and stocking them in inventory, you may still wish to consider stocking a few of your best selling items. Why you might ask would you ever want to do that? Well, there are actually a couple of very good reasons for doing so. The first will be to ensure that you have a reasonably continuous supply of those items, especially if they are from suppliers who do not have very reliable online inventory tracking systems. There will be much more on this later. The second reason is that most likely you will be able to get a better 'wholesale' price for those items.

It should come as no surprise to you that when you purchase items one at a time, as is the case with *Drop Shipping*, you will be paying more for your items than if you were to purchase the same products in bulk through normal wholesale channels. Either the 'drop ship' price you have to pay will be greater than the wholesaler's normal wholesale pricing, or there will be extra charges to pay, such as per-item drop ship charges, inflated S&H charges, or some type of membership fees. If anyone tells you otherwise, they are lying to you.

Not convinced? Then consider this for a moment. If that were not the case, then wholesalers which offer *Drop Shipping* as an option would have great difficulty selling their products in bulk through their normal wholesale channels. After all, what retailer in his right mind would ever want to purchase a truckload of a product from a wholesaler at the same per-unit price as another retailer could purchase just one unit of the same product? The answer should be obvious. No informed retailer ever would.

It is estimated that less than 10% of all products sold are in fact drop shipped, so that leaves the remaining 90% or more of product to be sold in bulk. To lose such a large chunk of that 90% would certainly not be a good position for any wholesaler to find himself in, but that is exactly the position which the wholesaler would be in, if retailers did not get more attractive pricing on bulk purchases, than they get on their non-bulk (drop ship) purchases. Thus there is indeed a 2-Tier pricing structure. Of course the sellers of the many so-called "Wholesale Drop Ship" lists and directories which are splattered across the Internet will try and convince you otherwise. They are misleading you.

False Claims Of List Providers

Many list providers claim to have an inside track on wholesale *Drop Shipping* channels, and thus are able to provide you with a seemingly endless supply of companies which are more than willing to drop ship their entire product lines to your customers, one item at a time, at or below their normal wholesale pricing. The sellers of such lists and directories are misleading you, as no such companies exist! They are trying to scam those uninformed enough to believe their false and misleading claims.

Such scammers are engaged in the business of selling

inaccurate and misleading information. Often their lists are comprised of nothing more than a few companies which they have copied and pasted from some Google or other engine search, often without so much as even clicking on any of the links provided to see if there are even websites at the other end, let alone making any attempt to determine if they at all fit the intended search criteria. Some lists do not even provide any links.

Recently I came across a very bad list being sold on eBay. It contained only company names, mostly PO Boxes for addresses, and no telephone numbers at all, let alone websites or e-mail addresses through which to contact the companies. I can't help but wonder that if I was gullible enough to waste my time and money in writing letters to the companies listed, just how many of my letters would have been returned as undeliverable for what ever reason.

In some cases, list sellers provide listings which consist mostly of companies where they have themselves signed up as affiliates. They hope to find buyers who are less informed than they ought to be, and fall for their misleading claims. They place ads claiming to offer listings of millions of items from numerous suppliers at 90% or more off the manufacturer's suggested retail prices. In all such cases, the products being offered have grossly inflated retail prices, and wholesale prices much higher than normal so as to allow the companies listed to be able to pay out affiliate commissions for any items sold.

Drop Ship Catalog & Website Scams

And finally, perhaps the biggest scam of all, are the so-called 'wholesale drop ship' companies which solicit the less-informed to sign up for either their own personalized drop ship catalog, or fully stocked online retail store. In exchange for a one-time set-up fee, ranging from a few dollars to several thousand dollars, and/or an ongoing monthly fee, would-be retailers will be provided with little more than a few overpriced catalogs, or an affiliate link to a replicated website. Such catalogs and websites are usually filled with nothing more than junk giftware-type items, or merchandise priced much higher than the going market price for such products.

Some of the more sophisticated scammers will pretend that they are setting you up with your very own custom online store. Some will even give you the impression that they are doing so under your very own domain name, but will require that you host your new site with *their* hosting company for an additional monthly fee.

One such company currently offers a number of different packages, with outrageous set-up fees ranging from $595 to $1795 depending on the set-up options chosen. This company even has the nerve to claim that their fees are actually discounted by approximately 60% from the normal selling prices of their packages. Yeah right! And I'm Santa Claus! In addition, on top of the above fees, if you wish your store hosted under your own domain name, you will be charged an additional domain registration fee of $15 annually (almost double the going rate), plus an additional $29.95 per month for hosting, which is now more than 4 times the industry norm for hosting such a site. In comparison, normal domain name registration costs just $8.95 per year at GoDaddy.com, while a *Deluxe Hosting Plan* with many more features than the one offered above for $29.95 per month, can also be obtained at Godaddy.com for ONLY $6.99 or less per month.

One company even tries to convince its potential victims that they will get a lot of traffic to their new store, as it will be submitted to over "700,000 Search Engines". That's quite interesting, since there are less than 100 Search Engines on the entire Internet.

What this company does is submit sites to numerous FFA links pages, which they falsely call *Search Engines*. The reality is that the likelihood of ever getting any *real* traffic from such postings will be slim to none. What you would get however is tons of e-mail spam, because that is the sole purpose of most links pages. They are set up to harvest e-mail addresses from those who try to post to them. Rarely will anyone ever actually see your links on such sites as they usually remain there for just a few seconds, if they are even posted there at all.

What potential retailers need to understand is that they will get nothing of any value for their money. They will receive only an affiliate link to a master website, or in the case of a hosted domain, perhaps a replicated website. Either way, the likelihood of ever selling any of the products offered will be extremely remote to say the least, as there will be hundreds, if not thousands, of members trying to promote the exact same over-priced products. And even more remote, will be the chances of ever making any money from it.

False Testimonials

Quite often you will find the sales and promotion pages of many so-called Drop Ship companies splattered with glowing testimonials from their so-called 'happy customers'. Sadly, the fact of the matter is that most testimonials and reviews for such services are fake. They are simply made up to try and convince the inexperienced into signing up for what ever it is those companies have to offer. In a like manner, often bad-mouthing and other criticism found in forums and blogs are not to be trusted.

What should be understood is the following:

1. People who give bad reviews, as you will often find in various blogs and forums, usually do so for one of two reasons.

    a. Either they got ripped off by the company in one way or another; or

    b. They are simply trying to degrade one program in favor of another...another that perhaps they themselves are promoting.

2. People who give good reviews for such services are usually associated with the company in one way or another. They are not real people [customers] so to speak. After all, consider this. If you found a great company to deal with, through which you could source all the products you needed to sell on eBay or elsewhere, why on earth would you ever divulge that info to someone else [your competitors] for free? Fact is...you would not! You would want to guard it with the highest degree of secrecy that you could. And you would certainly not want to encourage others to jump onto the same bandwagon you were on.

I do have to chuckle at some of the newbies who post to the eBay forums from time to time, seeking advice on where to find products to sell on eBay. While I suppose there is nothing wrong with asking, I would not hold my breath for any kind of a meaningful reply. From experience I find that most who reply do not know, and those who know, will not reply. After all, how would *you* expect a competitor to respond to such a question?

As a prime example, suppose I found the best source in the world for MP3 Players, which I intended to sell on eBay. How wise would it be for me to post that info for anyone else to see? To help my fellow sellers [competitors] make a lot of money too? Really? I don't think so!

But back to our topic of false testimonials. Such scammers rely mainly on the sale of their website packages, memberships, and catalogs as their prime source of income, rather than on the actual sale of the products they offer. And most will resort to any degree of lies and misrepresentation to reel in the naive. Unfortunately, the Internet is swamped with such scams. Beware of them, and beware of those who offer them.

Chapter 2

Drop Shipping Basics

What Is Drop Shipping?

Drop Shipping (or Dropshipping) is the term used to describe the process in which Company "A" purchases products from Company "B" on an "as-needed" basis. Then, rather than take physical delivery of the items purchased, Company "A" will have the items shipped directly to its customers from Company "B". That in a nutshell is the very "basic" concept of what *Drop Shipping* really is. Nothing more! Nothing less! How exactly the entire process unfolds however is what can either make you, or break you, in the retail drop ship business, especially if eBay is your prime sales frontier.

While the term *Drop Shipping* is a very simple concept, it is a term which all too often is widely misunderstood, and perhaps even more often, misused. As a retailer, not fully understanding the concept can not only cost you business, but it can indeed quite easily cost you *your* business.

If set up correctly, *Drop Shipping* can be one of the most lucrative of all retailing ventures which you as a business person could ever enter into. Set up incorrectly however, it can cause you more than a few headaches which you may not have anticipated.

It is my hope that after your have read this book, you will have a clear vision of just how the entire process should unfold, and that you will be much better equipped with the many tools necessary to reasonably ensure that it does.

25

Drop Shipper Lists & Their Providers

I think that it would be fair to assume that you are either already in the retail business, or have plans of going into that business in the not-too-distant future. I would also be willing to assume that you have already come across at least a few companies which either claimed, or were claimed by someone else, to be in the wholesale drop ship business. But then upon closer examination, you found that not to be the case. Perhaps you even bought a list or two in the past, only to be disappointed with what you discovered, for any of a number of reasons.

Outdated And Otherwise Useless Lists

If you did come across such lists, more than likely you found that most of the companies listed were not what they were claimed to be, if they even existed at all. Consider however, that a list many contain information on many fine companies, offering an excellent array of great products with the only problem being that the companies are not in the wholesale drop ship business. We should not however be too eager to condemn any of those companies, claiming false advertising or the like, as they may not even know that they have been placed on such lists. They may have simply been added there by a list provider who unfortunately did not bother to inquire as to what products and services the companies offered, or how they actually fit into the product supply chain.

Perhaps you have come across sites offering the greatest thing since sliced bread when it comes to wholesale drop ship lists. Indeed, there are a countless number of such sites (and auctions). Most of them claim to have lists of millions of products, from literally thousands of wholesale suppliers, all of whom are more than ready and willing to drop ship their entire line of brand name products directly to your customers, at an incredible 90% or greater discount off the MSRP (manufacturer's suggested retail price) of the products. Well let me tell you a little secret. No such suppliers exist!

If a company claims that it is an authorized wholesale supplier [distributor], and can sell you brand new authentic brand name products, drop shipped directly to your customers at discounts anywhere remotely close to 90%, RUN...don't walk away! And be very sure to hold on to your wallet very tightly while you are making your escape. The company is trying to cheat you in one way or another, just like it has likely cheated so many others before you.

Unfortunately, the providers of such lists have a zero degree of integrity. They put about the same degree of thought into scamming innocent people, as mosquitoes engage in before sucking blood from their next victims. Some of them are simply too lazy to even bother verifying the information they publish. As a result, they often end up distributing inaccurate and outdated information to list buyers. Others know very well what they are doing. They know that the information they are publishing (or re-publishing) is either false or not original, because they knowingly copied it from someone else without that party's permission. And again, they did not even bother to check it for any degree of accuracy. Yes, they even copied someone else's incomplete or inaccurate information, and are now attempting to pass it off as their own.

Not only are such scammers breaking every copyright law in the books, but they are providing their outdated and false information to those who were hoping to be able to rely on such information to help build their businesses. Instead, the buyers of such lists will only be helping to build the businesses of the scammers, with no chance of ever getting any return for their efforts, or for their investment.

Most of us no doubt have seen the hoards of eBooks and lists available on the Internet, where for just a few bucks, or in many cases for just a few pennies, you can not only get a copy of the eBook or listing for yourself, but you can acquire the "so-called" resale rights to do with it as you please. In other words, you can acquire the "rights" to sell them to others. Yes! For mere pennies, you can acquire the ability to sucker others in just as you would have been suckered in if you had bought such a list in the first place. The main problem with most of them is that the information they contain is useless. It is outdated at best!

Few will argue against the fact that very little value can be placed on information which was compiled and published 2 to 4 years ago, especially in a business in which, according to Small Business Trends, the death rate is 34% after just 2 years, and

56% after a 4-year period. Yes! It is estimated that within 4 years, 56% of all new businesses will cease to exist, at least in their original form. Some will argue that the failure rate is actually much higher, which I also tend to agree with. Nonetheless, if we combine even the more conservative mortality rates with normal changes necessary due to companies moving (i.e. change of address, change of phone number, change of e-mail, etc.), we should be able to imagine just how inaccurate any list would be after 4 years, and what little value it would really have. Such a list and $2.00 will get you a Starbuck's coffee. And yet those are exactly the quality of lists that you would get from the vast majority of list peddlers both on and off eBay.

Often many of the lists you will find on eBay, and elsewhere on the Internet, are nothing more than the results of a Google or other engine search which have simply been copied and pasted, without any care being given to its formatting, let alone the validity of the content being copied.

Experience will show that the results of such searches produce little more than links to other sites which, Surprise! Surprise!, have yet more lists for sale. Rarely will you find many companies which are what they are claimed to be. But if that was all you wanted, then you could have saved the money that you paid for this book, and done the search yourself. Then after spending a few months or more sifting through all the crap, contacting numerous companies to verify the contact information provided, validating telephone numbers, e-mail addresses, and so on, you would perhaps be able to come up with a half-decent list on your own. Few serious retailers, I think, have that much spare time on their hands, nor do they have the resources necessary in order to hire the help needed to do such research for them.

The Internet is swamped with such outdated and useless material, which among other things, often carry outrageous claims to be the best thing to ever hit online retailing. The sellers of such info often claim to have the golden goose. Some offers even come complete with a "No Questions Asked 100% Money Back Satisfaction Guarantee" to boot. But don't hold your breath! Such con-artists hope that you will get so swamped in sifting through all their garbage, that you will completely forget about their guarantee! While others are simply in it for the very short haul. They are in it to make a quick buck, and will more than likely not even be around by the time their customers discover that the info they bought is useless.

The Making Of A Good Drop Shipper List

In order for any supplier listing to have any real value, it must not only contain an extensive amount of information on each of the companies listed, but the information provided must be accurate. To accomplish that, it must not only be initially verified, but it must be updated on a regular basis. Providing only a name, address, and telephone number for any company will not do. While such limited information is of little value to begin with, as it tells you little of any value beyond that which you could obtain from any typical telephone directory, it becomes totally obsolete once it changes.

A "good" listing should provide most, if not all, of the following:

- **Full Name of Company** – The name provided should be the company's full operating/legal name, and not just a website name which often has little basis in reality, and certainly no basis legally.

- **Full Address of Company** – The address provided should be the full mailing address of the company, including the ZIP/Postal Code. After all, what good is any provided address if you cannot send mail to it?

- **Telephone Number** (Toll Free would be nice!) – If a listing does not provide a phone number to contact the company, or if you are not able to verify that the phone number provided is in fact valid, stay away from such a company, or you will regret it.

- **Fax Number** (If company has one) – With the popularity of e-mail, fax machines are being used much less. While at one point in time, fax machines were indeed used extensively to obtain quotations, submit orders, and so on, it is becoming more and more common that all those things are now being done using online forms and e-mail.

- **Website Address** – Generally you should be very aware of companies with either sub-domain URL addresses, or affiliate links. Most likely, companies which do not have their own domain names and websites, are not real wholesalers. Such sites, more than likely, are merely affiliates of other companies and are using replicated websites which were provided to them when they joined. Having said that, there are a few rare exceptions to this! A company may have been set up with an ISP years ago, at a time when private domains were not quite as popular as they are today. At that time, some companies were provided with free websites under a sub-domain arrangement. While the same is still offered today by many ISPs, such sites are rarely used for business purposes, the main reason being that they are impossible to transfer to another ISP should their owners wish to do so. If this is the case with a particular Company, the ISPs top level domain will normally be part of the company's e-mail address. (i.e. Suppose Company A has a sub-domain site hosted at AnyISP.com, the URL would look something like http://www.CompanyA.AnyISP.com or http://www.AnyISP.com/~CompanyA/ and the company's e-mail address would be something like CompanyA@AnyISP.com.

- **E-Mail Address** – If a listing does not provide either an e-mail address or a link to a contact form, or if you cannot verify the validity of the contact information provided, stay clear.

- **An 'About Us' Blurb** – It is always nice to know a little about the company you are dealing with, such as their origin, history, founders, and so on.

- **Product Categories** – This information should always be provided in order to give you a pretty good idea of what kind of business a particular company is engaged in.

- **Number of Products Carried** – This information is very important for two reasons. The first is that if a company only offers a handful of products which they do not manufacture, they are more than likely not wholesalers. No company can exist selling just a few different products unless either those products are very high end, or they sell a large number of them which would likely mean a great deal of competition. The second reason is that it will give you the ability to then determine the percentage of those products which are actually stocked. If less than about 80-90% of the items carried are actually stocked, the chances are that the company is not a real wholesaler.

- **Payment Methods Accepted** – Any listing should indicate the payment methods accepted by each of the companies listed. Any legitimate company will accept at least one major credit card either directly through its own merchant account, or indirectly through some payment processing system such as PayPal. If any company insists on only Wire Transfers, Money Orders, or Bank Drafts as payment....RUN!

- **Drop Ship Information** – Any listing should provide at least some information on each company's drop ship program. The more info provided...the better! It should be able to save you a lot of time. This is one of the most crucial areas of the entire listing which will determine if a company is in fact a wholesale drop shipper, or only pretending to be one. Unfortunately, 99% or more of all lists currently available do not have this information, which of course does explain quite a lot. Hint: The companies on such lists are not wholesale drop shippers.

- **Any Membership / Drop Ship Fees** – Any legitimate company will fully disclose all of its membership / drop ship fees up front, along with a full listing of its products, and how their respective wholesale prices will be calculated. If the company does not provide this information prior to you having to pay a set-up or membership fee, it is not a legitimate company. Any and all such fees required to join any company's drop ship program should be fully disclosed in any listing or directory.

A "great" listing will provide all of the above information, plus if the listing is in the form of an eBook or other online PDF/HTML based format, it will also provide hyperlinks directly to each supplier's website, product listing, e-mail address or contact form, and so on. Our Directory provides all this information and more for each source listed, which is why our

Directory is so widely recognized as one of the very best Drop Ship Information Sources available. (See offer on page 115.)

The Pros & Cons Of Drop Shipping

Like most aspects of doing business, *Drop Shipping* does have its share of pros & cons. If approached correctly, it should however be relatively easy to realize that the pros far outweigh the cons. If done correctly, *Drop Shipping* can indeed become a very lucrative business venture, for either the newcomer or the seasoned retailer.

PRO: Easy To Get Started

Setting up a new business, or expanding an existing one, is very easy to do. You can start today. All you need do is pick the products you want to sell, advertise them on your website, or list them on eBay or other auction site, and BINGO, you will be in the *Drop Shipping* business. Of course in reality, you should spend far more time researching the market for the products you wish to sell, and the companies you would like to purchase them from. You must ensure that you pick both the right companies, and the right products for *your* particular market.

Although somewhat tempting for many, it is not advisable to create just another online shopping mall. There are far too many of those on the Internet already, offering virtually every product under the sun. Very few potential customers take such sites seriously. Thus, the likelihood of ever selling anything worthwhile from any of them will be rather remote to say the least. And even more remote, would be your chances of ever making any worthwhile amount of money from it.

PRO: No Inventory To Carry

Perhaps the greatest advantage of *Drop Shipping* is the fact that you do not have to carry your own inventory. This gives you, the retailer, the ability to provide an almost unlimited variety of products with virtually no investment. You will not have to incur any of the usual expenses associated with inventory acquisition, such as incoming shipping costs, customs duties, taxes and so on. And of course, you will never have to worry about having any inventory on hand that you purchased at perhaps too high a price some time ago, or bear the risk associated with having a quantity of an item on hand that you cannot seem to be able to sell at any price.

I've been there and done that! So believe me when I say that it is anything but a pleasant experience to suddenly realize that part of your inventory is now obsolete, and that there appears to be no market for it at anywhere remotely close to what you paid for it. With *Drop Shipping*, this would never happen.

PRO: No Need to Package, Repackage Or Ship Items

Another great advantage of *Drop Shipping* is the fact that you do not have to spend time with unpacking, checking and repacking items that you would otherwise have to do if you purchased them in bulk. Nor do you have to spend time with any of the many aspects involved with preparing your items for shipment, especially if your customers are located Internationally, such as the preparation of customs documents, and so on. Someone else will do all that work for you if necessary, at a small price of course.

That price should be far less than having your own staff to do the same work for you, especially in the early stages of your business's growth. And if like so many other online businesses, you just happen to be a one-person operation, it will free up a tremendous amount of *your* valuable time that you can better devote to not only finding new products to sell, but in promoting those products which you have already found.

PRO: International Customer Base

Drop Shipping makes it very easy for you as a retailer to sell products to customers in many different countries, and do so without ever having to worry about any of the hassles associated with importing or exporting. All you need is a supplier who is willing to ship items to customers in your chosen country, while at the same time, deal with you (for payment) in your country. The most important factor which most suppliers will consider is the country you wish to ship to.

Most suppliers will want to be able to track the items they ship to your customers so that they will be able to provide proof of delivery in cases of dispute. This will be especially important to them for higher ticket items, and until such time as you have established a good working relationship with them.

If suppliers cannot track items shipped to a particular country, they will more than likely not want to provide you with *Drop Shipping* to that country, unless you have a proven track record with them, and are willing to provide them with a guarantee of payment, regardless of the outcome of such shipments. I do not recommend that you ever offer such a guarantee. This simply opens the door to potential abuse, with unfortunately you being the only ultimate loser in the deal.

Suppliers will not however be as concerned with the country from which payment is being made, so long as payments are made by a method, and in a currency which they accept. Most credit card processors, including PayPal, make this extremely easy these days, since they provide multiple currency payment and receipt options, and often do so all from within the same account, quite seamlessly, and at very attractive rates.

CON: Higher Wholesale Cost Of Products

It should not be at all surprising to discover that when you use a wholesaler's *Drop Shipping* service, you will more than likely be paying more (either directly or indirectly) for your products than you might otherwise have to pay if you purchased the same items in quantity through standard wholesale channels. So long as the difference is reasonable however, this should be expected, and fully acceptable. After all, you will be saving a great deal of money in other ways as we covered earlier, which should more than offset such an increase in costs. And of course, you will be completely eliminating all of the risks associated with carrying such items in inventory. Put another way, you should not reasonably expect to have it both ways.

CON: Limited Control Over Product Quality

In most cases, you will likely be listing and selling products which you have not even seen. As such, you may have only a slight idea from a picture what some items actually look like in the flesh, let alone be able to determine their quality (and thus their real value) as compared to the price you (and your customers) will have to pay for them.

If you are selling only Brand Name products from a reputable supplier, this should not be a problem. Plus, in some cases, you may even be able to see most if not all of the products at some local retailer before you decide if they are items you would like to offer.

If however you are offering less-known brands, you may not be able to find such products locally. That being the case, you would not be able to see what they actually look like, or get much of a feeling for their true retail values. This could present a very big problem. While a picture may indeed be worth a thousand words, seeing and handling an item will far outweigh any benefits which a photo would ever provide. There will be more on this later.

CON: No Direct Control Over Shipping

While the actual shipping of products is one of the most crucial aspects of *Drop Shipping*, it is the one aspect which can certainly present the greatest number of challenges for retailers. Unfortunately, it is also one aspect over which retailers ultimately have the least amount of control.

Other than perhaps choosing the carrier used, which even then is often pre-determined by destination, required delivery time, and costs involved, you may not have a very good handle on just how your items will be shipped, or when in fact, they will be shipped from your supplier. You will not normally know how your items will be packaged, how they will be handled in transit, or how they will be delivered to your customers. Having said that, it is indeed very important that you do get a good feeling for just what is happening here, and do so before you learn about it the hard way from customer feedback comments. This is especially important if you are selling your items on eBay where leaving feedback is considered such a big part of any transaction. But relax! Again, there will be much more on this later. There will be information on just what steps you can actually take to help ease any fears which you might otherwise have until such time as you are able to gain confidence in a particular supplier.

CON: Ordered Items Out Of Stock

Not unlike other companies, drop shippers sometimes do run out of stock of some of the products they carry. Unfortunately, when this happens, it can create big problems for you if you have not planned ahead for this. If a drop shipper runs out of stock of an item, it could result in you having sold and received money for items which you suddenly find that you cannot deliver. If you are selling your items only from your own website, this will not present as great a problem for you as it will if you are selling your items on eBay. There will be more on this in Chapter 4, under "Listing Items".

Some drop shippers provide a facility whereby retailers can check current inventory levels of an item. Some even provide a reserve option, much like a hold feature which can be placed on items at a typical 'bricks & mortar' store. While this reserve feature can certainly come in quite handy, it is not always 100% reliable. After all, as any business person knows, few inventory tracking systems are totally reliable, since inventory does seem to have a nasty habit of sometimes disappearing on its own.

Some of the larger drop shippers which cater mostly to high volume and auction sellers understand this problem very well, and will be much more facilitating to deal with such problems than perhaps some smaller drop shippers may be. This is where the importance of building a good supplier / retailer relationship will be most crucial, and perhaps put to the test. Regardless, you will need to find a way to smooth out the waters with *your* customers when this happens. You will not be able to simply make your customers wait until the items are back in stock, as this could take a very long time, if indeed at all.

Chapter 3

Selecting A Drop Shipper

Checking Status Of Drop Shipper

The very first thing you should do when considering any supplier, drop shipper or otherwise, is to make absolutely certain that they are an *authorized distributor* for the products you are interested in, and not simply pretending to be one. The key phrase here however is "products you are interested in". It is not uncommon for many suppliers to have received authorizations for some of the brands which they carry, perhaps even on an exclusive basis, yet carry a number of other brands which they obtain through some sourcing other than through that manufacturer's normal distribution network. In such cases, the supplier may very well be doing so contrary to that manufacturer's terms and conditions, but so long as you are not interested in those "other" products, this should not really be your concern.

You might be very surprised to know just how many companies do indeed claim to be "authorized" to carry a certain product line, when in fact they are not. Determining this supplier status up front is of particular importance when selling higher priced items such as those which come with warranties, or those which may require some type of support at some point down the road. Products which require firmware or software updates, and products which require ongoing replacement parts would certainly fall into such categories.

It is not at all uncommon for a manufacturer to either refuse to honor a warranty on items purchased through any channel other than its authorized dealer network, nor is it uncommon for them to deny support or replacements parts for such items. Nikon is one such company. Nikon Canada, for example, will not honor the warranty on any Nikon products unless they were in fact purchased from one of its Nikon Canada authorized dealers, nor will Nikon Canada offer any parts or support for such products. Nikon Canada even has the following warning to customers (Table 3-1) clearly displayed on its website, which addresses this very issue. There are many other companies which have adopted similar policies, even though they may not make them quite so visible to the public.

Important Notice To All Consumers — Beware of Purchasing Grey Market Nikon Products

It has come to our attention that certain Nikon branded photographic and digital imaging product is being imported and sold by unauthorized retailers, both over the Internet and in retail locations.

Please note that Nikon Canada is the only official authorized Canadian source for all Nikon branded photographic and digital imaging products. Nikon Canada distributes these products through a network of Authorized Nikon Canada Dealers. Always confirm that your camera retailer (whether electronic or 'bricks & mortar') is an Authorized Nikon Canada Dealer. Please consult the Dealer Locator for a list of Authorized Nikon Canada Dealers.

If you purchase Nikon branded photographic or digital imaging product from anyone other than an authorized Nikon Canada dealer, beware that Nikon Canada does not, and will not, provide parts, repair services, warranty service or technical support for any such product.

Nikon Canada only offers repair services or parts (including warranty service and technical support) for products purchased from one of its Authorized Nikon Dealers.

Table 3-1

Nevertheless, warranties and support issues aside, you should also consider that the more hands your products have to pass through before they get to your customers, the more they will cost you, and the less profit that you will be able to make on the sale. And of course, let's not forget, that the more hands your products have to go through, the greater will be the chances of something going wrong along the way, over which you will have little or no control.

If a company does not state on their website that they are an *authorized distributor* for a particular product line, more often than not, they are not. If on the other hand, they do claim to be authorized, do not simply take that as gospel. Assume nothing, no matter how nice or how professional you may think the people to be that you are dealing with. Check it out! This can usually be done very easily by visiting the manufacturer's website, as many manufacturers provide a listing of their distributors and/or dealers on their site.

If however the manufacturer does not provide this information on its website, or you are unable to find the name of your proposed drop shipper there, do not hesitate to contact the manufacturer directly, either by telephone or by e-mail. While the telephone will be much faster in many cases, either way, someone will be more than happy to confirm or deny any information you may have on a particular supplier. And in the event that your proposed supplier has not been authorized by that manufacturer, they will be able to provide you with the names of other distributors in your chosen area that you may not yet be aware of. In fact, here is a little secret. If you are already set on selling a certain brand of product, this is *the* place where you should always start.

Calling the manufacturer directly will take you all the way to the very top of the totem pole. While it will be very rare that you will find any manufacturer that will deal with you directly on a drop-ship basis, they should be able to put you in touch with one of their distributors which will. And above all, make absolutely sure that you make note of every name, every phone number, and every other little bit of information that you come across during your quest, no matter how insignificant you may think it to be at the time. At some point, it will likely come in very handy.

Physical Location Of Drop Shipper

It would be far more advantageous for your suppliers to be located in the same country as your customers, than it would be for them to be located in your own country (if the two are different). The reason for this is simple. As a seller, you should not expect your customers to have to incur extra expenses due to higher shipping costs, import duties, taxes and brokerage fees which they would not otherwise have to directly incur if they were dealing with a local retailer.

It is always advisable that your customers be made fully aware of the country (and even the state or province) from which their items will be shipped. eBay makes the process of doing this rather easy, since sellers have the ability to display not only their own *location*, but the *location* of the items they are selling. Unfortunately, this is also a feature of eBay which is often misused and abused by some sellers.

Some sellers neglect, often on purpose, to enter any meaningful information in the item *location* field. As a result, buyers end up being misled as to exactly where their items are coming from, and thus end up being very ticked off with the whole transaction, not to mention the fact that they usually end up having to pay far more to receive their items than they should have otherwise had to pay. The feedback profiles of several sellers I have come across are riddled with complaints regarding this very issue.

When used correctly however, as it was intended to be used, this feature can have a significant advantage for both retailers and customers alike.

- The advantage to you, the retailer, is that it allows you to sell to customers in another country or area, and have the items shipped to them from a local supplier.

- This will allow you to provide your customers with a more timely shipment of their items, as well as with the comfort of knowing that their shipment will not incur any unnecessary shipping costs, duties or brokerage fees.

- It will also be comforting for your customers to know that they will not have to handle any of the paperwork often involved with the importing of items directly.

Building A Partnership

When considering any drop ship supplier, it is of utmost importance to ensure that your drop shipper is at a proficient level of reading, writing and speaking *your* language. While there is often a certain degree of miscommunication in any business, a miscommunication problem due to a language barrier will rarely if ever be overcome. It will spell disaster. (No pun intended.)

During your supplier selection process, you should also make certain that either a good portion of their business is actually involved with *Drop Shipping*, or at least that they have a good understanding of the entire process. You should be reasonably assured that *Drop Shipping* is not simply an add-on service which they really intended to offer only on rare occasions through some special request process.

Sadly, I have come across several suppliers who in fact claimed to be well established drop shippers, but then after only a very brief conversation with them, quickly discovered that they really had little clue on even what the process was, let alone know how it should unfold.

Like you, your supplier needs to fully understand the entire process in order to ensure that everything runs as expected, and as smoothly as possible. You and your drop shipper must be able to form this bonding relationship if it is to work effectively. And make no mistake about it. This is a partnership. And like any other partnership, the success of the relationship requires a high degree of input and co-operation from both sides. If you fail to do your homework here, and forge a workable relationship from the get go, just like a poorly built marriage, it will not work.

Drop Shipper's Terms & Conditions

You will need to review fully, and very carefully, your selected supplier's *Drop Shipping* policy (assuming they have one), and be 100% certain that you are able to live within its boundaries and restrictions. You should know in advance all of the following. If all of the following are not fully disclosed, either in a formal *Drop Shipping* policy (Terms and Conditions), or elsewhere on the supplier's website, ask for clarification of any missing or unclear items, and do so before you spend a dime with that supplier. The following 15 sets of questions are not listed in any particular order, but they are all very important.

1. What fees (if any) does this supplier charge?

- Is there an account set-up fee? If "Yes", how much is it?
- Is there a monthly or yearly fee? If "Yes", how much is it?
- Is there a per-order or per-item fee? If "Yes", how much is it?
- If there is a membership or set-up fee, do they offer a free trial? If not, can you get a full refund within a certain time period should you find some part of the proposed relationship to be unacceptable?

NOTE: If any company insists that you pay a membership or set-up fee up front which is not refundable, and they want you to pay this amount before even seeing a complete product listing showing *your* actual costs for the items, including any shipping and handling charges, you would be wise to pass on that company. They are in the business of selling memberships and not products. Avoid such scammers!

2. Is there a minimum order amount?

- If "Yes", how much is it?
- If there is a minimum order amount, ask whether or not multiple items ordered at the same time, but going to different addresses, can still be combined to satisfy any minimum order requirements?
- If they do allow this "address" splitting of an order, make certain that you are fully aware of any additional fees which might apply, as well as any additional shipping and handling costs which may also be charged.

NOTE: If a supplier does have a minimum order requirement, this could present a problem for you, especially if you are selling lower priced items exclusively on eBay. eBay does not allow its sellers to impose any minimum order amounts, nor can you reasonably expect one customer to wait for his shipment while you sell additional items to other customers.

3. What shipping carriers do they use?

- Do you have a choice of carrier used for a particular shipment?
- What is the formula used for determining the shipping rates for each carrier?
- Are you charged actual shipping costs, or are they marked up to perhaps cover some otherwise hidden costs?
- If shipping costs are marked up, by how much are they marked up? Is it a set dollar amount? Or is it a percentage?
- Is tracking information provided in a timely manner, so that you can relay this information to *your* customers also in a timely manner?

NOTE: It is not uncommon for some couriers to charge a brokerage fee on International shipments, even when no duties or taxes are payable. While the brokerage fee itself is not a huge dollar amount, it can be quite a significant percentage on lower priced items. You would be wise to check with any courier being used as to their exact policy on this, along with their total shipping charges, before using them. At the same time, doing this will allow you to compare their actual rates to what your supplier is charging you for shipping and handling. It would certainly not be advisable to first learn of this from a few ticked off customers, who perhaps paid for a premium service, and received anything but.

4. What payment methods do they accept?

- What credit cards do they accept?
- Do they accept PayPal?
- Other methods of payment accepted such a wire transfers, money orders, etc. although I would strongly advise against the use of any of those in this business.

NOTE: If you intend to use PayPal to pay your supplier, you will need to make certain that your supplier has no problem shipping to alternative shipping addresses. After all, do not forget, that it is you who will be paying your supplier, but the items must be shipped to your customers. If however you accept PayPal as payment, and hopefully insist that your customers have "confirmed shipping addresses", then indirectly, the items will be shipped to your customers' confirmed addresses. You will however still need tracking information from your supplier in order to resolve any delivery disputes which may arise.

5. When does your supplier ship?

- How long after payment is received before your order goes out the door?
- Does your supplier close for any holiday periods throughout the year beyond normal statutory holidays? It is not uncommon for some companies to actually close, or at least cut back operations during Christmas/New Year and/or March Break, and perhaps for a 1-2 week annual vacation.

NOTE: You will need to add this turnaround time to your own in-house turnaround time when providing your customers with shipping and delivery time estimates. If any supplier does not normally ship within 2-3 days of payment receipt (weekends and holidays excepted), it may be wise to pass on that particular supplier, unless you are prepared to state on your auction page or website that such items will be shipped within "X" business days, and provide a reasonable explanation for such a delay. Also, if your supplier closes for holidays, you will need to plan your auctions around this period.

6. Does your supplier stock all the products they offer?

- If "No", you will need to find out which items they stock (or do not stock), as it would not be advisable to offer any non-stocked products on any kind of a drop-ship basis, and certainly never for any eBay auction.

NOTE: If you find that a particular supplier does not stock many (or any) of the products they offer, this should be a good clue that they are most likely not an authorized distributor for those products. They may in fact be having such items shipped to them from another company on an as-needed basis, or perhaps even drop shipped for them. In reality, you could very well be buying products from a drop shipper who in turn is buying from another drop shipper. Do your homework, and avoid such an arrangement.

7. Is it possible to check in-stock levels at any time?

- If "Yes", how? (i.e. online, telephone). Is such a system relatively reliable? Ask! Can you reserve items?
- If "No", how can you be reasonably assured that the item you are selling will be in stock when you wish to have it shipped to a customer? The fact is, you cannot.

NOTE: If you are unable to check a supplier's inventory level for an item, and the supplier does not provide a facility whereby you can place a reserve on an item, again you would be wise to avoid using that supplier, especially if you intend to sell your items on eBay. And also, you have to be relatively comfortable that any inventory numbers you are provided with are reliable. Here is a disclaimer provided by one supplier which I came across recently:

> "The stock listed above does not take into account any products which may be on hold for customers, or for any stock variances which may happen from time to time."

In short, such a disclaimer renders the inventory information provided virtually useless.

8. Does this supplier accept retailers from *your* country?

- If "Yes", make certain that you are fully aware of the currency accepted by your supplier, and that you are able to pay them in that currency.
- Make certain that you fully understand the exchange rate for your supplier's accepted currency, if it is different from your own.

NOTE: Do not confuse this with the "countries" to which a supplier ships. There are many drop shippers in the USA for example who will ship only to USA addresses, due to tracking problems involved with shipping to other countries. This does not mean however that they will not accept retailers from *other* countries. In fact, many of them will.

9. Does this supplier ship to the country in which you would like to have customers?

- If "Yes", make certain that your supplier is able to provide you with tracking information for the items shipped, especially if you are dealing in higher priced items.

- If "No", you would be wise to indicate such 'country' restrictions on your auction pages for those items.

NOTE: You will need to determine this before you list any items for sale on eBay. If your drop shipper does not ship to a certain country, you will need to do at least one of the following: a) block such auctions from bidders in that particular country; b) state in your auction that you do not ship to country "x"; or c) have the items shipped directly to you, so that you can re-ship them to your customer. Of course, this latter option will add to your overall expenses, as well as to total shipping time, so this arrangement may not be viable.

10. What about PO, APO and other such "box" address deliveries?

- Does your supplier ship to all types of "box" addresses?

- If "No", you will need to either make a notation on your auction pages that you do not ship to certain types of "box" addresses, or else you will need to have such items shipped directly to you so that you can then re-ship them to those customers affected.

NOTE: You should be aware that while your supplier may have no problem shipping to PO or APO boxes, your delivery options will be limited. Most couriers do not ship to *any* "box" addresses. So if your supplier does not ship to PO or APO Boxes, you will need to clearly state this fact on your auction pages. Also, if using PayPal, you should be aware that while PO box addresses can be confirmed, members using APO Boxes will most likely not have confirmed shipping addresses, although I see no real problem here. From experience, I find those in the Armed Forces (APO Boxes) to be among the most honorable on this planet.

11. Does your supplier identify themselves in any way to your customers? Do they include a packing slip with the shipment?

- Will the supplier use your shipping labels (if you send them some in advance)?
- Will the supplier produce labels with your name (and address) on them as the shipper?

NOTE: You will need to make certain that if your supplier does include a packing slip with the order, that it does not identify your supplier as the seller. While most drop shippers will normally include packing slips with orders, they will not have any prices showing, nor will they identify themselves to your customers. Bear in mind however, that if your supplier is exporting your items to another country, they will need to provide the proper customs documentation with the parcel. This obviously could present a problem for you, since there will need to be some value indicated on it. While this may be one very good reason for having your drop shipper located in the same country as your customers, it is something which you will need to work out in advance with any supplier that you choose to export products.

12. What about this supplier's Return Policy?

- Do they offer refunds?
- If "Yes", how much do they refund?
    - Full amount paid
    - Amount paid <u>less</u> S&H charges
    - Amount paid <u>less</u> S&H charges <u>less</u> a restocking fee
- If "Yes", does this supplier require that a RMA number be obtained before a return will be authorized or accepted, and must that RMA number be included on or with the returned item?

NOTE: Most companies will not refund S&H charges unless the return is due to an error they made. It is also not uncommon for many companies to charge a restocking fee on returns unless again the item is being returned due to an error they

47

made. In virtually all cases, you will need to first obtain an RMA number from your supplier before returning an item, have that number included on or with the return, and have the item shipped using a service which provides tracking. In any event, your return policy should be exactly the same as your supplier's return policy, unless of course, you are willing to: a) have the items returned directly to you; b) issue a refund to your customer; and c) either try and re-sell the item, or return it to your supplier yourself.

13. What about defective merchandise?

- What is this supplier's Warranty Policy?
- Do items come with a valid manufacturer's warranty? (They should if they are from a manufacturer's authorized distributor.)
- Where does the item have to be shipped if something goes wrong? (i.e. To the manufacturer, To the supplier, To a repair depot)

NOTE: Your customers will need to be made fully aware of your supplier's policy on this for each item you sell, unless of course again, you are willing to make some alternative and direct arrangements with your customers, such as an extended or alternative warranty provision, etc.

14. Does this supplier sell to the end user (your potential customers)?

- If "Yes", what is their pricing policy?
- Do they sell to the public only at the MSRP of the items? Or can anyone buy products from this supplier at the same price you have to pay? If the latter is the case (as it sometimes is), have nothing to do with that supplier, as you will not be able to compete with them, no matter what you do.

NOTE: A good rule of thumb to follow in any business is to never try and compete with your supplier. Or put another way, never buy from your competitor, which in this case, would also be your supplier. *You* will most always lose!

15. Does this supplier sell any products directly on eBay, or on any other auction site that you wish to sell on?

- If "Yes", again it would be wise to have nothing to do with them. As before, you would simply not be able to compete.

NOTE: It would be wise to search your chosen auction site for any items you wish to sell there before listing them. This will not only give you a pretty good idea of who, if anyone, is selling them, but it will also tell you where they are being sold from (i.e. country?). And of course, it will give you a pretty good idea of the going price you can expect to get for such items. Again, do your homework, as it will save you countless hours of needless frustration.

Chapter 4

Choosing, Pricing & Listing Items

Choosing Products

Often one of the hardest decisions facing any retailer, is choosing which products to offer, since not even the largest of mega-stores can realistically offer them all. Looking through the myriad of products available can indeed be quite overwhelming, even for the most seasoned retailers. The initial experience can be much like that of a young child in a candy store. So many products, and so little time!

The good news is that unlike doing business in a typical 'bricks & mortar' environment, making a few mistakes in the *Drop Shipping* business will not be quite so costly. In fact, even if you make a number of mistakes in the products you choose, you will at least not end up with a warehouse full of them, for which you cannot find buyers. Nonetheless, if you are to be successful in this business, you will need to focus on just what it is you want to accomplish. You will need to discover the best products to offer to your chosen market, and you will need to learn how to market those products most effectively.

If you intend to sell your products primarily on eBay or other similar *semi-closed* online marketplace, you will need to try and choose those products which will have the least competition. And of course, you will also need to choose those products which will provide you with the best profit margins. After all, making a profit is the name of the game, is it not?

Another major consideration when choosing products will be the actual shipping costs of the various items. Since selling online is essentially a modern form of mail-order business, both sellers and buyers must consider the shipping costs of the products being offered. After all, there would be little value in saving $20 on an item which could be purchased locally for $50 if it costs $20 or more to have the item shipped. This is very typical of lower end consumer electronics, as well as various stereo components, TVs, etc. Often such items appear to be real bargains, but then after considering the high cost of shipping, not to mention the possibility of damage in transit due to the nature of the items, they are quite often no bargain at all.

While it might seem that almost every product imaginable can be found on eBay at one time or another, you should not necessarily shy away from a little honest competition. Even if your competitor is buying his items in bulk through normal wholesale channels, you should not have a hard time competing with him, since your overhead expenses should be a great deal less than his.

If however there is a large difference between your minimum selling prices, and those of your competitor, you should try and find out why. One of 4 things is likely taking place:

1. Perhaps you have set your target selling prices too high. Keep in mind that the MSRP of an item often has no correlation to its realistic selling price. There will be more on setting prices in the next section.

2. Perhaps you are paying too much for your items. Some drop shippers do indeed price their items way too high as compared to their normal bulk wholesale pricing. You will need to be very careful with this one. As explained earlier, while you should expect to pay more for your items when you have them drop shipped, than if you were to buy the same items in bulk, the difference should be reasonable. Do not assume that you are getting a good deal on an item simply because the supplier claims a discount of "XX" percentage. Often the MSRP is inflated by suppliers to make it look like larger discounts are actually being given.

3. Perhaps your competitor is not purchasing his items through normal authorized wholesale channels. This happens a lot, especially in the consumer electronics market, and even more so on auction sites such as eBay. If you *are* authorized to sell a particular product line, then you should clearly state that fact in your auction descriptions. Remember that potential buyers have the ability to check you out, just as you have the ability to check out your potential suppliers.

4. Perhaps your competitor is not being honest when he states that his items are brand new. Unfortunately, unscrupulous sellers will often claim items to be brand new, when in fact they are not. They will try and pass off returns, repackaged, and refurbished/remanufactured items as being brand new. Over time, this unethical practice should be reflected clearly in a seller's feedback profile.

Yes, unfortunately there are a number of dishonest sellers on eBay, just as there are a number of dishonest sellers in many areas of the 'bricks & mortar' world. While it may be very hard over the short run to compete with a dishonest seller, over time honesty will win out. Remember however that you are not purchasing any inventory, except perhaps for a few of your already time-proven fast sellers, so it will cost you very little beyond eBay's nominal listing fees to try many different things. This is also an excellent way to utilize eBay's many special offers, such as their $0.05 - $0.20 listing days which they have from time to time. So plan ahead!

Keep in mind that experienced buyers will consider a lot more than just price when selecting a seller to buy from. A seller's location, feedback reputation, page design, product photos, item description (including grammar and spelling), payment methods accepted, and stated terms and conditions, will all play a part in the seller selection process. More often than not, good sellers with higher prices will win orders that not-so-good sellers with lower prices do not. The best way to compete in any business, just as in any aspect in life, is to be better than the competition. Selling on eBay is no exception to that rule.

As a retailer, you will need to know as much as possible about the products you offer, so as to be able to correspond intelligently with your customers when they ask questions. Some buyers will ask questions before they place a bid or make a purchase, while others will have after-sale questions and concerns which will need satisfactory replies. You will need to be prepared for both.

If you think that you can simply wing your way through this, trying to adlib as you go, or perhaps by even ignoring questions for which you have no real answers, you may want to think again. This business may not be for you. With such an attitude, you would most likely not do very well at it, certainly not on eBay. And if the poor feedback reputation you would receive did not quickly end your eBay sales career, the number of credit card or PayPal chargebacks you would likely get by ignoring after-sales problems, surely would.

As a retailer, it will be necessary for you to view yourself as your customers will view you. And to apply the Golden Rule, you will need to treat your customers as you would like to be treated. Otherwise, the outcome will not be at all desirable.

Setting Prices

It would be wise to do a considerable amount of research before actually selecting items to sell, and certainly before setting their selling prices. While you should not get too greedy, neither should you needlessly cut yourself short of any profits that you might otherwise be able to realize. If you set your prices too low, many will assume that there is something not quite right with your particular items, and avoid your auctions, especially if your reputation is less than ideal.

In a like manner, if your items are not in factory new condition, you should not attempt to mislead your customers that they are better than they really are, solely to get a higher price for them. This will surely come back to haunt you, and faster than anything else, will kill your eBay reputation. Set your prices at a reasonable level as compared to that of your "real" competition, for the exact type and the condition of the products you are offering. Experience will be your guide.

Fixed Price Listings

If you intend to use eBay's *Fixed Price* listing format to sell your items, your "Buy it Now" prices should be set at least 10-15% above your actual product costs. Plus you will need to show additional amounts for S&H, based of course on the destinations your items will be shipped to. All of your order processing and shipping expenses should be incorporated into your total S&H charges, as opposed to including them in the base selling price of your products. This will have at least two distinct advantages:

1) It will save you a little on the Final Value Fees which eBay charges upon successful completion of auctions, since eBay does not currently charge commissions on S&H amounts; and

2) It will make your items appear a little more competitive, since many buyers focus primarily on the bid amount of an item, and not so much on the S&H amounts charged, even though in reality, price comparisons should really be comparing only the *total* amounts which buyers have to pay.

Keep in mind however that according to eBay rules, the amounts sellers charge for S&H *should* be "reasonable". This is actually covered under the section in eBay rules titled "Circumvention of eBay fees". eBay unfortunately does not provide any specifics on just what constitutes "reasonable", which I suspect is why it does not appear to enforce that rule, except in the most extreme of cases, such as the listing of items with a "Buy it Now" set at only $1.00 or less, and a grossly inflated S&H amounts many multiples that of any actual shipping costs.

Should you somehow get the idea that you can offer $100.00 items by listing them for just $1.00, and then charging buyers $99.00 S&H, you may wish to re-think that notion. While you might get away with it for a short while, doing so will not only adversely affect your overall feedback reputation, but it will eventually get you in trouble with eBay, especially when other members complain about you. And they will.

When eBay acts on such complaints, as they often do, it will usually result in your auctions being removed without notice. For more extreme or repeated cases however, you could very well end up with your eBay account being indefinitely suspended. If that happens, your eBay days will likely be over, as getting back on eBay after such a suspension, or at least staying there for very long, is not an easy thing to accomplish, as so many have discovered the hard way.

In any event, it would be wise to calculate your total S&H charges for each item in advance, and either clearly display those amounts on each of your auction pages, or alternatively, provide an online calculator with which your potential buyers can calculate their own amounts before bidding on your items. From experience, I find that grossing up actual shipping costs (postage or courier fees) by 1.5 to 3 times should adequately cover both your actual shipping cost and your handling expenses. You should also find that very few if any will complain, either to you or to eBay, about such reasonable charges.

Standard Auction Listings

If you are using eBay's *Standard Auction* listing format to sell your items, then you should consider setting your minimum starting bid at least 10% above your cost. Then perhaps have an optional "Buy It Now" set at least 10% above your minimum starting bid amount. If you end up with no bids after 3 or 4 listings, drop the item because it is not a good seller for you at this time.

If however after 3 or 4 listings, you end up getting only the minimum bid amount each time, and you are not happy with that amount, you might want to try either raising the minimum bid amount, or else lowering the "Buy It Now" amount to see if either makes any difference in the final price you get. Also, until you are sure that you have a good selling product, or are content with just your minimum bid amount, it is not wise to list multiple auctions for the same item. From a buyer perspective, there would be no incentive to "bid up" an item, which they more than likely will be able to win for just the minimum bid amount if they wait a little longer.

Most sellers who list several auctions for the same identical item, rarely get more than their minimum bid amount. On rare occasions, they may sell the odd item through the "Buy It Now" option, but again there is no incentive for buyers to use that option, since they can usually wait and eventually obtain the item at only the minimum bid amount. Some sellers are obviously very content with this, as they list numerous auctions for the same item. Such sellers do however often have grossly inflated S&H charges, so they obviously make their money that way. So do what ever works best for *you* and *your* particular items.

While the margins I have suggested may seem low to some, especially to those with a 'bricks & mortar' background, remember that when *Drop Shipping*, they do provide pure profit. Such margins should actually provide more profit than you would achieve selling the same items for the same amounts, if you had purchased them through conventional wholesale channels, and now held them in inventory. That is of course assuming that you are getting reasonable wholesale prices from your supplier.

Listing Items

eBay Listing Policies

If you are planning to sell your products exclusively from your own website, then obviously none of eBay's policies will apply to you. If however you are planning on using eBay as a marketing venue, then you should read the following section very carefully.

Before listing any items on eBay, I would strongly suggest that you familiarize yourself completely with eBay's List of Prohibited [banned] and Restricted Items, and with all eBay rules regarding the listing of such items. You should be aware of what items may not be listed on eBay under any circumstances (Prohibited Items), and what items may be listed there, but which require certain steps to be taken in order for such listings to comply with the guidelines set for the listing and sale of certain items (Restricted Items). Failure to follow these rules will result in your auctions being removed. Repeat violations will result in account suspension. The following is a listing of items which may affect you:

Prohibited and Restricted Items: (eBay.com)

- Adult Material (see Mature Audiences)

- Alcohol (see also Wine)
- Animals and Wildlife Products - examples include live animals, mounted specimens, and ivory
- Art
- Artifacts - examples include Native American crafts, cave formations, and grave-related items
- Catalytic Converters and Test Pipes
- Cell Phone (Wireless) Service Contracts
- Charity or Fundraising Listings
- Clothing, Used
- Coins
- Contracts
- Cosmetics, Used
- Counterfeit Currency and Stamps
- Credit Cards
- Drugs & Drug Paraphernalia
- Drugs, Describing Drugs or Drug-like Substances
- Electronics Equipment - examples include cable TV de-scramblers, radar scanners, and traffic signal control devices
- Electronic Surveillance Equipment – examples include wiretapping devices, and telephone bugging devices
- Embargoed Goods and Prohibited Countries - examples include items from Cuba
- Event Tickets
- Firearms, Weapons and Knives - examples include pepper spray, replicas and stun guns
- Food
- Gift Cards
- Government and Transit Documents
- Government and Transit Uniforms
- Government IDs and Licenses
- Hazardous, Restricted, and Perishable Items - examples include batteries, fireworks, and Freon
- Human Parts and Remains
- Importation of Goods into the United States - examples include CDs that were intended only for distribution in a certain country
- International Trading
- Items Encouraging Illegal Activity - examples include an eBook describing how to create methamphetamine
- Lock-picking Devices
- Lottery Tickets

- Mailing Lists and Personal Information
- Manufacturers' Coupons
- Mature Audiences
- Medical Devices - examples include contact lenses, pacemakers, and surgical instruments
- Multi-level Marketing, Pyramid and Matrix Programs
- Offensive Material - examples include ethnically or racially offensive material and Nazi memorabilia
- Pesticides
- Plants (see Weeds and Seeds)
- Police-Related Items
- Political Memorabilia
- Postage Meters
- Prescription Drugs
- Prohibited Services
- Real Estate
- Recalled Items
- Slot Machines
- Stamps
- Stocks and Other Securities
- Stolen Property and Property with Removed Serial Numbers
- Surveillance Equipment
- Teacher's Edition Textbooks
- Tobacco
- Transit and Shipping Related Items - examples include blueprints of transit facilities, airplane operations manuals, and flight attendants' uniforms
- Travel
- Weeds and Seeds
- Wine (see also Alcohol)

Prohibited and Restricted Items: (eBay.ca)

- Alcohol (see also Wine)
- Animals and Wildlife Products - examples include live animals, mounted specimens, and ivory
- Art
- Artifacts - examples include Native American crafts, cave formations, and grave-related items
- Catalytic Converters and Test Pipes
- Cell Phone (Wireless) Service Contracts
- Charity or Fundraising Listings

- Clothing, Used
- Coins
- Contracts
- Cosmetics, Used
- Counterfeit Currency and Stamps
- Credit Cards
- Drugs & Drug Paraphernalia
- Drugs, Describing Drugs or Drug-like Substances
- Electronics Equipment - examples include cable TV de-scramblers, radar scanners, and traffic signal control devices
- Electronic Surveillance Equipment – examples include wiretapping devices, and telephone bugging devices
- Embargoed Goods and Prohibited Countries - examples include items from Cuba
- Event Tickets
- Firearms, Weapons and Knives - examples include pepper spray, replicas and stun guns
- Food
- Gift Cards
- Government and Transit Documents
- Government and Transit Uniforms
- Government IDs and Licenses
- Hazardous, Restricted, and Perishable Items – examples include batteries, fireworks, and Freon
- Human Parts and Remains
- Importation of Goods into the United States - examples include CDs that were intended only for distribution in a certain country
- International Trading
- Items Encouraging Illegal Activity – examples include an eBook describing how to create methamphetamine
- Lock-picking Devices
- Lottery Tickets
- Mailing Lists and Personal Information
- Manufacturers' Coupons
- Mature Audiences
- Medical Devices - examples include contact lenses, pacemakers, and surgical instruments
- Multi-level Marketing, Pyramid and Matrix Programs
- Offensive Material - examples include ethnically or racially offensive material and Nazi memorabilia
- Plants (see Weeds and Seeds)

- Police-Related Items
- Prescription Drugs
- Prohibited Services
- Real Estate
- Recalled Items
- Slot Machines
- Stamps
- Stocks and Other Securities
- Stolen Property and Property with Removed Serial Numbers
- Surveillance Equipment
- Tobacco
- Transit and Shipping Related Items - examples include blueprints of transit facilities, airplane operations manuals, and flight attendants' uniforms
- Travel
- Weeds and Seeds
- Wine (see also Alcohol)

In addition to having a basic understanding of the items you can and cannot list on eBay, you should also fully understand eBay's VeRO Program (Verified Rights Owner Program), and how that program may apply to the products you wish to sell.

eBay VeRO Program

The eBay VeRO Program is essentially an agreement made between eBay and its VeRO members, for the purpose of protecting their intellectual property rights. The VeRO Program's membership consists of a number of companies and individuals who either strictly forbid any of their items from being listed on eBay, or have specific requirements on just how such items may be listed, or how any of their intellectual property may be used.

As a seller, you will need to know which companies and individuals are members of the VeRO Program, and how their policy may relate specifically to your products. Be aware that eBay will automatically remove all auctions which violate the rights of its VeRO Members, and will quickly suspend sellers for repeat violations.

Highlights of the VeRO Program include:

- Removal of listings reported to eBay by more than 5,000 intellectual property rights owners.
- Proactive monitoring and removal by eBay of listings that violate eBay's policies designed to prevent the listing of infringing items.
- Ability to save searches and have the results emailed to you through Favorite Searches.
- Suspension of repeat offenders.
- Cooperation with rights owners seeking personal information on alleged infringers.

Again, the VeRO Program either completely restricts certain items from being listed on eBay by those not specifically authorized to list such items, or else it provides very strict terms and conditions under which such items may be listed.

Contrary to popular belief, no seller has any right whatsoever to sell any product for which the product's manufacturer, or rights owner, has not granted the seller a specific right to do so. Nor does any seller have the right to use any trademark, or copyrighted material, without first obtaining permission from the holder of such rights to do so. Obviously what you do from your own website can not easily be controlled. What you do on eBay however most certainly can be, and will be. Furthermore, eBay will provide your personal information to those whose rights you violate, so that they may take any necessary legal action against you, if they so choose to do so.

Make no mistake about it. Failure to abide by eBay's listing rules will result in any auctions which violate such rules to be removed from eBay without warning. Subsequent violations of the same, or different rules, will eventually result in suspension of your account. Generally, eBay works on an escalating penalty system. Such penalties range anywhere from an informational e-mail alert for a first-time minor violation, to a formal warning or account suspension for more serious or repeat violations.

Account suspensions can range in time, anywhere from just a few days for lesser violations, to being indefinite for more serious infractions. A member's past history, and the severity of the rule broken, will be what will ultimately determine the actual penalty received.

Item Descriptions

Be accurate! Describe your items as fully and as accurately as possible. If your items are brand new, then state that fact. If however they are not new, then state that fact also.

If you are selling brand new items, it is best to provide the manufacturer's exact description of the item (no more! no less!), paying particular attention to what is included in the box, and what is not. For example, if an item runs on batteries, but does not come with any batteries, state that batteries are not included. Of course if batteries are included, state that they are.

When selling new items, it is perfectly acceptable to use the manufacturer's stock photos of that item, provided of course that the manufacturer does not have any problem with your use of its graphics. Do not however provide a photo of model "x" of a product, when you are in fact selling model "y", even thought you may otherwise very accurately describe the item you are selling. Inappropriate photos of an item are misleading at best.

If you are selling remanufactured, refurbished, reconditioned, or used items, then state your items as being exactly as they are. Again, provide accurate descriptions of the items you are selling. It is of course still perfectly acceptable to provide the manufacturer's description of the item, however you should bear in mind, that certain accessories, features, warranties, and so on may no longer apply to such "non-new" items. The item's description should therefore be adjusted accordingly. And above all, unless the item is *exactly* as the item would have been in brand new condition, do not use a stock photo. Instead, take a photo of the actual item you are selling, and note any changes, additions, deletions or flaws which a brand new item would not have.

Most buyers will read your item descriptions and take them quite literally, as of course they should. If your descriptions are vague, some buyers will ask questions for clarity. Some may assume such and such to be the case, and ultimately blame you when they make the wrong assumption. But most buyers will simply avoid vaguely described items completely.

If your auctions state that something is included, buyers will rightfully assume that it is. So rest assured, that what you say, or in some cases, what you do not say, will most certainly come back to haunt you if you are wrong. And remember that while some customers may indeed be very unreasonable, that is no reason for you as a seller, to be equally unreasonable. Two wrongs do not ever make a right!

Shipping & Handling Charges

As previously discussed, it is always advisable to either fully disclose your S&H charges directly on your auction page, or else provide an online calculator with which your customers can calculate their own charges. I personally find that stating S&H charges directly on the auction page works much better, as there can be no dispute later, since eBay archives all auctions for at least a 90-day period after their close.

While providing an online calculator is certainly much better than nothing at all, it does leave the door wide open for a buyer to later claim that the amount he is being charged at checkout is not the same amount as he was quoted when he checked prior to bidding. There could be a number of reasons for this:

- Perhaps he misread the displayed quote;
- Perhaps he entered a wrong zip or postal code during his quote inquiry;
- Perhaps he is confusing your auction with one from another seller; or
- Perhaps he just enjoys playing such games with sellers.

Regardless of the reason, if and when this happens, you will likely not be able to provide your buyer with any kind of an explanation that he will find acceptable. Of course, if you have set up your auctions using eBay's Fixed Price format, and require immediate payment upon purchasing, this will not be an issue for you.

Regardless of which method you choose, providing such info will go a long way towards eliminating, or at the very least reducing potential arguments with your buyers over your S&H charges which they do not think are reasonable. Believe me! It is far better for a buyer to pass on your auction because he thinks you charge too much for S&H, than it is to have a buyer who refuses to pay for an item because you tell him the S&H charge is $X after he has already won your auction. The latter is a recipe for disaster, or at least an easy way for you to obtain negative feedback.

Insurance

Contrary to a common belief which many sellers have, whether or not your customers actually choose to pay an additional amount for insurance, as a seller, you are still 100% responsible to ensure that the items your customers pay you for, are delivered to them in "as advertised" condition. If the items you ship become damaged or lost in transit, then it is your responsibility as seller to take up any issue of claim with the carrier (or shipper) involved, and ensure that your customer is either compensated for the damage or loss, has his item replaced without charge, or gets a full refund. No exceptions!

While you are certainly within your rights to disclose any amount you have to pay to insure the items you ship (or have shipped), doing so will not change your responsibility as seller. eBay provides the following options with regards to how you disclose your insurance policy for each auction you list:

- Not Offered
- Optional (with amount showing)
- Included in S&H Amount
- Required (with amount showing)

Contrary to popular belief, a seller is under no obligation to pay a courier or postal service to insure an item, even though he may have included an insurance amount as part of the total S&H amount charged. A seller is well within his rights to self-insure any items shipped, as in fact many companies do. Self-insurance simply means that the seller assumes 100% of the risk of shipping.

Also contrary to popular belief, it is not up to the recipient of an item to file a claim for loss or damage with the respective carrier. The total responsibility for filing such a claim rests with the seller (shipper). If an item is lost or damaged in transit, the recipient should contact the seller and inform him of the problem. The seller in turn should then file the appropriate claim with the respective carrier if insurance was purchased, or take care of the matter on his own if he self-insured the shipment. Either way, it is the seller's sole responsibility to ensure that the buyer is compensated 100% for the loss or damage, and do so regardless of whether or not the buyer actually purchased any insurance offered. How the seller ultimately resolves this matter with the carrier is really of no concern to the buyer. Of course, the buyer will be expected to show proof of damage to the carrier (if carrier insured), or to the seller (if self-insured).

In most if not all cases of loss of, or damage to, insured items, payment from the respective carrier will be made directly to the shipper, and not to the intended recipient of the item.

Terms & Conditions

All of your auctions should include a copy of your Terms & Conditions, indicating most if not all of the following:

- **Payment Methods You Accept:** i.e. PayPal, Credit Cards, Money Orders, Checks, etc. While these are all payment options which you will be given the opportunity to select when listing your items on eBay, it is a good idea to also state them in your Terms & Conditions.

- **Payment Methods You DO NOT Accept:** i.e. Personal Checks. It is not a good idea for any seller to accept personal checks, especially from buyers in another country. If you are in Canada for example, you should know that US Checks can easily be returned "NSF" or "Account Closed" 30 days or longer after you deposit them, which will most likely be long after you have shipped your items. And to make matters even worse, you will not only be out the cost of your item, plus the amount you paid for shipping it, but you could also be out a considerable amount due to currency exchange costs and returned check fees. When (not if) this happens to you, sadly you will find that there will be next to nothing that you can effectively do to get your money back.

- **How You Ship:** i.e. Postal Service (USPS, CanadaPost), Courier Service (UPS, FedEx, etc). It would be wise to select only a service which provides on-line tracking of your shipments. If not, you will find that it may indeed become an insurmountable problem should any dispute be filed against you for non-receipt of an item.

- **When You Ship:** i.e. Within "X" business days of payment receipt. The period selected should not normally exceed 2-3 business days unless you are offering a "pre-sale" item, and if that is the case, you should clearly state that fact in your auction description.

- **Local Pick-up Options:** i.e. If you do not allow local pick-up, you should state that fact. Or if you do allow pick-up, then you should indicate that pick-up is available only between the hours of 00:00 and 00:00 EST (your local time), Monday thru Friday, and whether arrangements need to be made beforehand, etc.

- **Shipping Restrictions:** i.e. No PO or APO Boxes. If you do not wish to ship to PO or APO Boxes, you should state that fact. Also you should bear in mind, that most couriers will NOT normally ship to any "Box" addresses, so you will need to use the Postal Service if you want to ship to customers using box addresses.

- **When Payment Is Due:** i.e. Within "X" days of an auction's close. I think you will find that the longer the time period you allow here, the less will be your chances of actually getting paid. I would recommend 3 days maximum. From experience, I find that 80% of buyers pay for items either immediately, or within 24 hours of an auction's close, and of those who do not pay within 72 hours, a staggering 80% do not pay at all, even after unpaid item disputes are filed against them.

67

- **Return Policy:** i.e. Do you offer refunds, or are all sales final? If you do offer refunds, state the conditions under which a refund will be given, and the formula for calculating the amount to be refunded. State also your policy for exchanges. Do you require RMA numbers for returns? If so, state that fact.

- **Hours of Telephone Operation:** i.e. This is very important if you provide a phone number for buyers to contact you with any questions or problems they may have, unless of course you have a good answering system, and plan on returning their calls later.

- **Your Sales Tax Policy:** i.e. If you charge Sales Tax to customers in certain areas, you should indicate that fact on each auction page, along with the actual percentages charged for each jurisdiction.

- **Your Feedback Policy:** i.e. That you always return feedback after your buyers have received their items, are happy with them, and have left the appropriate feedback for you. Some sellers do this, while others do not. Some argue that stating such a policy may drive away some buyers. Perhaps, but you would more than likely not want the ones you will drive away by openly stating such a policy.

- **Your Non-Paying Bidder Policy:** i.e. That you always file an UID (Unpaid Item Dispute) against those buyers who bid on and win your auctions, but then for what ever reason, decide not to pay.

Delivery Time Estimates

Be sure to provide adequate delivery-time estimates to your customers. In fact, it is always better to over-estimate here, than it is to under-estimate. Your customers will most likely be thrilled if they receive their items early. They will not however be very happy campers if they have to wait for their items much longer than you told them it would take for their items to reach them.

Some buyers tend to be very unreasonable with this one. Some buyers feel that sellers somehow have total control over the items they ship every step of the way, even though no reasonable person would ever think that a seller has much control over items once they have been placed for delivery with the Postal System, or some courier services.

In any event, the bottom line is: Play it safe, and it will reap many benefits for you. Promise the moon however, while delivering only a pebble, and needless headaches will no doubt soon be coming your way.

Out Of Stock Items

If your chosen drop shipper does not offer a reserve feature as covered in Chapter 2, then you will certainly need to be prepared to deal with the fact that sooner or later, you will sell an item and find it to be out of stock when you go to place your order for it. When this happens, you will need a definite plan. In an ideal world, of course you would have another in-stock source for an identical item. But since this is not an ideal world, we both know that will most likely not be the case.

Some sellers will include in their item descriptions that they reserve the right to cancel an auction if the item becomes no longer available, or that they reserve the right to refund payment for the item if it is found to be out of stock after the auction closes. eBay only partially supports sellers in this.

While eBay does provide a facility for sellers to cancel auctions for such reasons, it does so only up to a point. Sellers must cancel their auctions prior to the last 12 hours of an auction's run. Within the last 12 hours however, sellers are not able to cancel their auctions for any reason. So unless you are lucky enough to find out that the item you have listed is out of stock before those last 12 hours, the option to cancel will not be available to you.

While some sellers do state that they reserve the right to refund payment for items which they find to be "out of stock" after the auction closes, neither buyers nor eBay look very kindly on this. Quite often, this is seen to be nothing more than an unethical ploy on the part of sellers to get out of having to sell an item for a lower price than they had anticipated getting for it. Of course, that argument would not apply to auctions which closed using the "Buy it Now" option, since the Buy it Now amount would obviously be the seller's desired closing price for the item.

Regardless of any underlying reason for wanting to cancel an auction, just as an auction is considered to be a contract binding upon the winning bidder to make payment, so too does it bind the seller to deliver the item sold. Of course in reality, no seller can be expected to deliver something which he does not have. The seller will however be expected to smooth out the waters as much as possible, to satisfy both the buyer and eBay.

While of course nothing is guaranteed to ever completely smooth out the waters for an unhappy customer, there are things which you can (and should) do that will go a long way towards that end. And if you are lucky, they will even help you avoid getting negative feedback in the process. Looking closely at the past feedback of your buyer should give you a very good feeling of just how receptive he will be to any of your offers.

1. Immediately after you discover that the item you sold is out of stock, contact your supplier by telephone to make certain that the item is in fact out of stock. If it is, try and get an update on whether or not new stock is expected, and if so, precisely when it will arrive.

2. Determine if there are any reasonably close in-stock alternatives to this item. Ideally, any alternatives should be at least as good, if not better than the original item. If there are alternatives, place a hold on 2 or 3 of the closest ones, if you are able to do so with this particular supplier.

3. Determine if you are able to get the exact same item, or close alternatives, from another source.

4. Only after you have done all three of the above, should you consider contacting your customer. After all, it may not even be necessary to do so if you have correctly followed steps 1 thru 3. Besides, there is no need to sound an alarm before the fire starts. Should however the need exist for you to have to contact your customer, then the very first thing you must do is apologize for *your* blunder. Yes! *Your* blunder! You must admit that you made a terrible mistake. Buyers will appreciate this very much, and will be much more receptive to any suggestions which you may present, than if you simply make excuses, and try to blame someone else for what has happened.

5. Offer your buyer all of the "options" you came up with in steps 1 thru 3 above. Your presentation of options should ideally include all of the following, if available:

    a. Give your customer the "Option" to wait for new stock which should be arriving on "date". Provide him with the actual expected date. You should not however expect your customer to wait more than a week to 10 days longer than he would normally have to wait to receive his item. You may however be able to speed up this waiting time a little by giving your customer a free delivery service upgrade (i.e. Overnight, etc). Also, you should offer to compensate your customer for having to wait. State your offered compensation amount at this point. It should be at least equal to him getting "free" shipping or 10% of the item's selling price, which ever amount is greater. Bear in mind however that the new "date" you give must be reliable. It will be up to your supplier to convince you that it is, and perhaps even compensate *you* if he is wrong. You'll well need it if he is wrong, because you will be wrong yet again with your customer.

    b. Offer your customer his choice from 2 or 3 of the closest alternative items from your list, assuming there were some. And assuming they are all more expensive than the original item, be sure and point out this fact to your buyer, but do not under any circumstances attempt to charge him any extra for an alternative, no matter what the actual difference is. If you do, most buyers will see this as simply a bait and switch ploy to sell higher priced items from the start. At that point, all they will want is a refund. In addition to shipping an alternative, you should also offer to refund the shipping charge he has already paid as a little extra compensation.

    c. Finally, offer your buyer a full refund, plus an additional 10% or $100.00, which ever is less, as compensation for his time. Do not worry! You would be very surprised on just how few will actually take the offer of a refund.

In addition, you would be very wise to try and assure your buyer that you do indeed appreciate his business very much, and that you are truly sorry this has happened. You may also wish to bring his attention to your excellent feedback reputation, with the key word here being *"excellent"*. Unfortunately, if you do not have a fantastic feedback reputation, this whole process will likely not work well for you. It would be seen as a scam by many buyers. And that being the case, you would be best giving the refund, otherwise a chargeback would likely follow, perhaps without even contacting you.

It might also be a very good idea to remind your buyer of other options available to him through PayPal or his credit card company should you not live up to your end of the bargain. This could also help ease the fears of an otherwise suspicious buyer who at this point, may very well view you and your actions as being somewhat less than honorable.

If you follow all these steps exactly, you will not only be reasonably assured that you will not receive a negative for this transaction, but you may even receive a positive for your *superior* customer service. With experience, you will be able to refine this process rather well. It works! Use it!

Chapter 5

Payment Methods

Are You Losing Business?

As indicated in Chapter 1, merchants who do not accept credit cards or PayPal as payment options, are likely to suffer greatly in their overall online sales volumes. This is particularly true if their prime sales avenue is eBay. In fact, accepting credit cards or PayPal has been found to increase the sales volumes of typical eBay sellers by as much as ten times that of sellers who do not. According to eBay, 90% of eBay sellers now accept PayPal as a method of payment for their auctions, and that by doing so, they reduce their overall non-paying bidder numbers by as much as 70%.

Most eBay buyers will not purchase items unless they have the ability to pay for them using either their credit cards, or their PayPal accounts. With the amount of fraud taking place online these days, buyers do need to be reasonably assured that when (not if) something goes wrong, they will have the ability to get their money back. Paying with a money order or bank wire transfer will not provide them with that ability, since using either of those payment methods is virtually the same as sending cash in the mail. Such payment methods do not provide buyers with any degree of protection.

Furthermore, it should not be at all surprising to know that the vast majority of sellers who insist on being paid with money orders or wire transfers are indeed scammers. They are either not likely to deliver anything that they sell, or else they will deliver items which are considerably different from those described in their auctions. Such sellers of course realize that their buyers will not be pleased, and will want to get their money back. They also know very well that once they have cashed their money orders, or received their wire transfers, that their buyers will have little or no recourse available to them.

Oh sure, there are those who claim that the Postal Service will take action against those who use money orders and the mail to commit such fraud, as will the banks sometimes take action against violators. But that is often only an illusion...a false sense of security. In reality, the chances of scammed buyers ever getting their money back will be far less than it would be for them to get hit by lightning three times in a row, on a completely dry Sunday afternoon in mid July. Well maybe not quite that rare, but the odds of doing so will not be at all good, since according to a recent CNN report, less than 1 in 700 cases of fraud are ever fully investigated, and of those which are investigated, the chances of getting money back are very slim.

Of course at this point, you may be wondering what all this has to do with you, since you are a seller, and not a buyer, right? Well let me assure you that it does indeed have a lot to do with you, for two very important reasons:

1. When your buyers' confidence levels fall, as they will no doubt do if you do not provide your buyers with adequate payment methods which will protect their interests, so will your overall sales fall; and

2. While you may consider yourself a seller, you will most likely be someone else's buyer, whether on eBay or elsewhere.

Merchant Accounts & Credit Card Services

The term *merchant account* is quite often misunderstood. While many assume that merchants who accept credit cards directly from their websites, or for their online auctions, all have their own merchant accounts, in reality they do not. What most merchants are doing is simply using a *credit card service* which provides them with only some of the benefits associated with accepting credit cards directly. Of course, some of you may wonder just what the differences are. Well there are indeed several very distinct differences which any merchant should become fully aware of before ever considering using such a service. Failure to fully understand the risks involved could very well be far more costly than you could ever imagine.

These are the major differences:

1. A true *merchant account* will be in the name of the merchant (you), whereas an account with a *credit card service* provider will actually be using a *merchant account* which will be in the name of that particular provider. This often makes it difficult for customers to recognize charges on their credit card statements, especially in cases where there were currency conversions made. This results in unnecessary chargebacks.

2. *Credit card service* providers usually charge a much higher discount rate to process credit card payments than are charged by banks for typical merchant account transactions. In addition, most providers will charge set-up fees (usually in the $100s of dollars), ongoing monthly and transaction fees, check issuing fees, and so on. Most providers will also charge a substantial fee for every chargeback which you end up receiving, and some will even charge you for providing customer refunds, on top of the fact that you were already charged a commission on the initial transactions, which often will not be refunded.

3. With your own merchant account, you can usually get your money immediately. Your credit card receipts can be transferred directly into your bank account as soon as they are processed daily, or at least as soon as you deposit the bank copies of your credit card sales slips into your bank, should you process payments manually.

4. With most *credit card service* providers, you will not receive your money immediately as you would with your own merchant account. In fact, many providers will send you a check only once or twice monthly. Some will even hold back a percentage of the amount owing to you for an additional number of billing periods,

sometimes as long as 6 months, as security against the possibility of future chargebacks.

5. Cre*dit card service* providers will go to any lengths to protect *their* merchant accounts. They would much rather lose you as a customer, than take any chance of losing one of their merchant accounts. As such, they will not under any circumstances tolerate a very high number of chargebacks. In fact, after just a very minimal number of chargebacks, you may well find your account suspended or even terminated. Once this happens, you may find that even the amount that you are legitimately owed at that point may well be placed on hold for an extended period of time.

6. If one of your customers complains to your cre*dit card service* provider for virtually any reason whatsoever, and asks for a refund, it will be given to him. This is of course in keeping with # 5 above, in that such providers will go to any lengths to protect their merchant accounts from chargebacks. They will immediately assume (and rightfully so) that if a customer complains to them, asks for (or demands) a refund and does not get one, a chargeback will follow. Thus they give refunds often without question. After all, it is not their money that they are returning now, is it? In many such cases, you would not even be contacted except to advise you that a refund was given. You would really have no say in the matter.

The fact that you may have just shipped a $1000 digital camera or a laptop computer to your customer would likely not influence the provider's decision to give the refund. Not only would you be out at least your cost of the camera or the computer, but quite frankly, there would likely be very little if anything that you could do about it. You may not even have the real name or the real address of the customer you shipped the item to. In fact, the credit card used to purchase the item may very well have been stolen. But one thing is for certain...It is your money that the *credit card service* provider just helped some scammer steal from you.

After carefully considering all these comparisons, one might ask: Why on earth would any online merchant ever want to use such a service, instead of simply getting their own merchant account? Well, the fact of the matter is that a true merchant account can sometimes be very difficult to obtain, especially when used exclusively for online sales.

It can also be very difficult for a new business to obtain its own merchant account, unless the owner has a well established credit record in good standing, and is perhaps willing to either personally guarantee any charges which his company may incur, or else place a substantial amount on deposit as security against future chargebacks. Thus, those who are new in business, or those with poor credit, would more than likely have a very uphill battle in satisfying the merchant account requirements of their respective credit card issuing institutions. Until PayPal came along, merchants had little choice. Now they have a choice!

PayPal

With a PayPal account (depending on account type), in addition to enjoying standard member-to-member instant money transfers, you will be able to accept most major credit cards, as well as eChecks. You will also enjoy features comparable to, and in many ways better than those offered by typical merchant accounts, or other payment processing facilities, and all at very competitive rates.

With a PayPal account, there are no set-up charges, no monthly charges, and no gateway fees as charged by typical merchant accounts and credit card service providers. In fact, payment processing, fraud protection, and numerous tools to enable you to accept payments online, either for your online auction sales, or for your own website transactions, are all included in PayPal's very low transaction costs.

When you accept PayPal, you will also be opening your door to a network of over 100 million PayPal users worldwide. Those active online shoppers transact an average of $8.1 billion USD per quarter, and this number is growing daily, as more and more members come to realize the value and security that only a PayPal account offers.

Types Of PayPal Accounts

PayPal offers three different account types:

- Personal
- Premier
- Business

Each account type has access to a different set of features and capabilities.

Personal Accounts

Personal Accounts are for use by individuals only, and can receive a total of only 5 credit card payments.

Personal Account holders do however have the ability to pay for items using their credit cards.

Personal Accounts include all Core Features (see below).

Premier Accounts

Premier Accounts are for members who have a high transaction volume, and either need to accept credit card payments, or would like access to special features which a Personal Account does not provide.

Premier Accounts include all Core Features, as well as a number of Premium Features (see below).

Premier Accounts may operate under an individual name.

Business Accounts

Business Accounts are for business use only.

Business Accounts include all Core Features, as well as all Premium Features (see below).

Business Accounts can operate under a company or group name.

Core Features:
- Send Money
- Request Money
- Auctions Tools

- Website Payments
- Money Market
- Virtual Debit Card
- Account Insurance
- Downloadable Log
- Email-based customer service

Premium Features:

- All Core Features
- Do business as yourself, or under a corporate or group name
- Accept unlimited credit card payments
- Payment Receiving Preferences
- Subscriptions
- ATM/Debit Card
- Mass Payments
- Multi-User Access for Business Accounts
- Advanced Downloadable logs
- 7 day-a-week toll free customer service

Business and Premier Accounts are assessed a small transaction fee ($0.30 USD), plus a low discount rate (1.9 – 2.9%) based on your previous month's volume. Even for lower volume sellers, this discount rate is usually much lower than those charged by typical merchant accounts, especially given the fact that with PayPal, there are usually no additional transaction fees, no monthly fees, no statement fees, and no bank transfer fees.

There is however one small additional fee which PayPal calls a "cross-border" fee. That fee is very similar to the conversion fee charged by most credit card companies, and applies only to transactions in which a currency conversion is necessary, such as when US Sellers accept Canadian currency to be deposited into their USD accounts. The fee has been waved for Canadian sellers.

There are no fees involved for receiving payments to a Personal Account. But while this may sound like a tempting option, remember that with a Personal Account, you are able to accept a total of only 5 credit card payments, after which time you will need to upgrade your account in order to continue receiving payments by credit card.

Other Payment Processing Services

While there are indeed many different payment processing services available on the Internet, all claiming to offer their members more than the others do, there is not a lot which can be said about any of them which has not already been said. We have already covered the basis on which most typical services operate, as well as the many pitfalls associated with using such services.

The fact of the matter is that if you use such a service, you will likely lose a considerable percentage of your money to scammers, as the service provider will not be there to help you in times of dispute. In other words, when disputes arise as they often do from time to time, the service provider will more than likely take the side of the buyer in order to protect its own account standing, and as a result, you as a merchant will be left out in the cold with no money, no product, and in most cases, no recourse.

Scammers understand fully just how these services operate, and will often target those merchants who use them. Buyers know very well that they can purchase products and services, receive them, and then either charge back their credit cards, or get refunds simply for the asking. They know that they can often get refunds directly from the service provider with virtually no questions asked...refunds which will in turn be charged back to you, the vendor, usually with no chance for you to argue your case. Is that the kind of a company you would like to deal with as a seller? I would hope not.

Protection For Sellers

No other financial institution does a better job at protecting its members than PayPal does. By employing a large team of experts in virtually all areas of online safety, and utilizing the very latest in secure technology, PayPal continues to be a world leader in safe and effective online payment processing. Again this fact is well evidenced by PayPal's rapid growth to its current membership base of over 100 million accounts worldwide.

PayPal vs. The Competition

PayPal takes steps to protect its members in ways that many other financial institutions do not. For example, credit card companies often charge for their fraud prevention tools. At PayPal, you'll find that many of the same tools are available for free. And not only that, but unlike many of its competitors, PayPal's fraud prevention experts work behind the scenes, monitoring account activity for possible fraud indicators, to help ensure an extremely safe network within which its members can conduct their business.

Should any suspicious activity occur in your account, a PayPal representative will alert you either by email, or by telephone. But PayPal does not stop there. PayPal also offers excellent chargeback protection, unmatched by most other financial institutions.

Many credit card companies frequently put buyers' needs before those of its merchants. This means that when chargeback disputes occur, it often becomes an uphill battle for sellers to reach any kind of a satisfactory resolution, since they usually have little if any say in the matter. This is due mainly to the fact that online merchants do not normally have the buyer's credit card in hand at the time of the transaction, nor are they likely to have obtained the buyer's signature for the charge. Thus proving the validity of a transaction is very difficult at best. This is one of the greatest hazards facing online merchants today, and one which unfortunately many traditional banking institutions have not yet come to grips with, or taken any steps to resolve.

PayPal, on the other hand, is equally concerned about all of its members. That is why, should a buyer file a dispute, PayPal will act as a mediator between both parties. Often this results in a resolution before a chargeback is ever filed. If however mediation does fail, and the buyer files a chargeback, PayPal will use evidence provided by the seller to fight any fraudulent chargebacks. This will be where your shipment tracking and/or delivery confirmation information will be required. If you cannot provide proof of delivery, you will unlikely be able to reach any kind of a satisfactory resolution.

In these and other ways, PayPal offers a uniquely comprehensive level of protection for sellers, not offered with typical merchant accounts.

Fraud Prevention

State-of-the-Art Technology

You can count on PayPal's state-of-the-art technology to help keep your transactions and financial information safe and private. By using the most advanced encryption methods available, and constantly improving on existing technology, PayPal has built its reputation as a leader in privacy and identity protection. In addition, PayPal's highly sophisticated fraud prevention models alert them to suspicious account activity to which its dedicated team of anti-fraud professionals are trained to immediately respond.

PayPal also provides industry-standard AVS and CVV2 checks as additional layers of identity theft protection, in addition to package tracking integration so as to further decrease chargeback risk.

The Anti-Fraud Team

PayPal's Anti-Fraud Team works 24 hours a day, 7 days a week to help keep your sensitive information private. Using sophisticated risk models and advanced technology, the PayPal team is able to detect, and often predict, suspicious activity to help eliminate identity theft. The Anti-Fraud Team's sole function is to make every PayPal transaction as safe and as seamless as possible.

More ways PayPal decreases fraud risk:

- Cooperation and shared investigations with the FBI and other law enforcement agencies
- Educational resources, including how to prevent chargebacks, protecting yourself against identity theft, and seller safety tips

Perhaps this is as good a place as any to encourage you to read very carefully Chapter 6 (next chapter) on Identity Theft.

In that chapter, you will not only learn the meaning of both Phishing and Spoofing, but you will discover how to make sure that it does not happen to you.

The Resolution Center

PayPal's Resolution Center facilitates fair and speedy resolutions of disputes between buyers and sellers. A dedicated team of specialists will help resolve a dispute before a chargeback is filed, and will do so free of charge. Should dispute resolution fail, PayPal will work with you to fight a fraudulent chargeback, and help you protect your money.

You can track PayPal's progress in any dispute at their online Resolution Center on the PayPal website. Plus the Resolution Center's online submission feature is particularly convenient if PayPal asks you to submit evidence to help win your case, such as tracking/delivery information for the item you shipped, and so on.

No seller wants to be caught in a buyer dispute, but if it does happen, you can count on PayPal to walk you through the resolution process step by step.

The Resolution Team

If a buyer files a dispute with PayPal through its online Resolution Center, PayPal's Resolution Team will review and help both buyer and seller work toward a satisfactory resolution, so that the buyer does not file a chargeback. In many cases, this mediation process can resolve a dispute quickly and fairly so that both parties feel satisfied. PayPal is the only online financial service that provides arbitration to its members free of charge.

If arbitration fails and the buyer decides to follow through and file a chargeback against you, PayPal is there to help. PayPal's specialized team will review your case and work with you to ensure that you have the best possible chance of winning a fraudulent chargeback. PayPal will ask you for information regarding the transaction and use it as evidence when disputing the chargeback with the credit card company. You're much more likely to win a fraudulent chargeback dispute with PayPal's team of experts on your side. Plus, you'll save time and frustration by letting them handle most of the work.

And what is even more, if the disputed transactions qualify to be covered under PayPal's Seller Protection Policy, you will be covered for up to $5,000.00 USD per year.

Chapter 6

Identity Theft

Phishing & Spoof E-Mail

If you are not yet fully aware of the meaning of the word *phishing*, and how it applies to you, then I would strongly suggest that you read this chapter very carefully before you do another thing, as your very financial future may indeed depend on it.

Phishing is the term given to that area of identity theft, in which the victim is persuaded through one of a number of different means, to provide crucial ID information regarding one or more of his personal accounts, financial or otherwise.

Phishing usually takes the initial form of spam e-mail. The targeted victim will receive an e-mail which upon first glance, may appear to come from PayPal, eBay, or some other similar organization where the targeted victim has an account. The e-mail may have any of a number of subject lines, from a very generic one such as "Account Suspended", "E-Mail Address Added", and so on, to a very specific one, perhaps even referencing one of your actual eBay auctions, or PayPal transactions.

The e-mail will usually start out with something like "Dear PayPal Member" or "Dear Customer". It will then go on to identify some "urgent" matter needing your immediate attention, such as there being a problem with your account, or that a new e-mail address has been added to your account, etc.

The proposed solution in the e-mail will be for you to either click on the link provided in the e-mail and update the required account information at the web page you would be taken to, or else reply to the e-mail with the requested account details, such as verification of your account ID and password, etc.

The problem with such e-mails is two fold...

1. The e-mail you received was a spoof. It did not originate from the organization claiming to have sent it to you.

2. The site you would visit, if you were to click on the link in the e-mail, would not be the site you would think that you were visiting, even though it would probably look identical to your particular organization's "real" website.

Know this! Both the website and the e-mail address were set up for the sole purpose of obtaining valid account information from those who fall victim to this scam. If you were to ever provide your account ID and password information to such a site, or in a reply to such an e-mail, you would find that your account would be very quickly hi-jacked, and you would no longer have any access to it. Furthermore, any funds which were in it at the time, would be instantly removed. Hi-jacked eBay accounts are used for another reason, such as the sale of non-existent products. But that is really beyond the scope of this book.

In any event, it would be very unlikely that you would ever get any money back that you would lose to such a scam. Nor would you likely be able to undo any damage done to your eBay account. The main problem would be that it would be *you* who gave the scammer *your* information. There would be little or no evidence of the scammer actually stealing it from you in the traditional sense of the word, nor did he obtain it through some other source. You must fully understand that it is your sole responsibility to protect your eBay or PayPal account ID information, just as it is your responsibility to protect any other login information, or your ATM PIN number. And while of course there are laws intended to protect victims of such crimes, just as there are certain actions which a victim may take to try and resolve such situations as they occur, the final outcome is rarely satisfactory. As a victim, you would always lose. The trick is to not become a victim in the first place. And that includes not playing the role of the victim as so many often do, by trying to blame someone else for their own mistakes.

If you ever receive an e-mail with a generic salutation such as "Dear eBay Member" or "Dear PayPal Member", know that the e-mail did not come from either of those companies. Neither eBay nor PayPal will ever send such e-mails. Both companies always personally address the recipient in any e-mails they send, such as Dear "*Your Name*" (real name and not simply your eBay ID), and they will never ask you to provide any personal information in an e-mail reply, nor ask you to click on any link in an e-mail in order to provide any of your account information.

Reading E-Mail Headers

One of the best ways to determine if the origin of an e-mail is authentic, is to examine the e-mail's header. There are several ways of doing this. Here is one excellent, and most effective way.

- Within one of the header's "Received:" fields will normally be a line containing the acronym "HELO" (short for *Hello*), or in less frequent cases, the acronym "EHLO" (short for *Extended Hello*).
- The "HELO" or "EHLO" line will be inside the *first* of two sets of brackets.
- Immediately following the word "HELO" or "EHLO" will be the actual domain name (website) from which the e-mail was sent.
- Within the *second* set of brackets will be the sender's corresponding IP address.
- If there is either nothing or else garbage within one or both sets of brackets, the header field has been forged, meaning that the e-mail did not come from the place from which it is claimed to have come.

Following are a number of examples to illustrate some of the different scenarios which could occur:

Example 1

Subject: Notification of payment received

Received: from 216.113.188.112 (HELO outbound2.den.paypal.com) ([216.113.188.112])

The above information is from an authentic e-mail which came from PayPal.

Example 2

Subject: eBay Item Sold: # XXXXXXXXXXXX

Received: from unknown (HELO mx66.smf.ebay.com) ([66.135.209.201])

The above information is from an authentic e-mail which came from eBay. Note that it is not uncommon for the word "unknown" to be used in place of the actual IP address immediately following the word "from".

Example 3

Subject: Message from eBay Member Regarding Item # XXXXXXXXXXXX

Received: from 212.67.42.121 (EHLO new.ctc.fr) (212.67.42.121)

The above information is from a spoof e-mail. The e-mail did not come from eBay as the subject and body of the e-mail would suggest. In this case, the spoof e-mail originated from a server in France.

Example 4

Subject: PayPal Suspension Notice

Received: from 200.232.127.234 (HELO terra.juresa.com.br) (200.232.127.234)

The above information is from a spoof e-mail. The e-mail did not come from PayPal as the subject and body of the e-mail would suggest. In this case, the spoof e-mail originated from a server in Brazil.

Example 5

Subject: CitiBank Account Flagged

Received: from unknown (HELO 200-171-161-18.dsl.telesp.net.br) (200.171.161.18)

The above information is from a spoof e-mail. The e-mail did not come from CitiBank as the subject and body of the e-mail would suggest. In this case, the spoof e-mail originated from a server in Brazil.

All e-mail coming from eBay or PayPal will have their actual domain information within the "HELO" or "EHLO" bracketed field (First Set), and their IP Address within the second set. So in other words, if you do not see something to the effect of "ebay.com" or "ebay.ca" after the "HELO" or "EHLO" line, the e-mail did not come from eBay. And likewise, if you do not see "paypal.com" within the HELO or EHLO line, the e-mail did not come from PayPal.

The most important thing to understand here is just how actual domain name information is assembled. One way is authentic, and the other completely fake. The actual "domain" from which the e-mail is being sent will be at the very *end* of HELO or EHLO string contained within the first set of brackets. It will not be anywhere else within the string. Here again are some examples of this:

Example 1

(HELO mx66.smf.ebay.com) - This is an example of a possible domain information string. Note the "ebay.com" at the end of the string. This site would reside on an eBay server.

Example 2

(HELO outbound2.den.paypal.com) - This is also an example of a possible domain information string. Note the "paypal.com" at the end of the string. This site would reside on a PayPal server.

Example 3

(HELO mail.ebay.rogers.com) - This is an example of a possible domain information string which would not reside on an eBay server. In fact, in this case, the domain information string would reside on the rogers.com website. Note the "rogers.com" at the end of the string. So you see why it is so very important to examine this aspect of an e-mail header's information very closely.

Example 3 illustrates a very common trick used by spoofers to mislead those who receive their fake e-mails. Another very common trick is for spoofers to actually register domain names as close as possible to the sites they wish to replicate, such as e-bay.com, eebay.com, paypal1.com, and so on. The point is that all such sites are fake. They have been set up for the sole purpose of gathering actual login information from members of the targeted organization, who sadly are often less informed than they ought to be.

While there is a considerable amount involved with reading and understanding e-mail headers, it is a skill that anyone can master with experience. Plus, there are often other ways in which you can often verify the authenticity of any e-mails you receive, but that in itself could fill a book, and unfortunately is not the intended focus of this one. So my advice at this point would be to play it safe, and heed the warnings.

For additional information on spoof e-mails, especially as they relate to eBay accounts, I would recommend *eBay's Spoof E-Mail Tutorial* located at http://pages.ebay.com/education/spooftutorial/ or in Canada at http://pages.ebay.ca/education/spooftutorial/

Account Hi-Jacking

In the unfortunate event that you find that your financial or other account has been compromised in any way, you should contact your respective institution immediately. In the case of eBay, you should contact eBay at http://pages.ebay.com/help/confidence/isgw-account-theft-reporting.html or if you are unable to access your eBay account, through eBay's *Live Help* system.

As stated on eBay's website, eBay recommends that you take the following actions:

> First, check with family members and others who may use your account to verify that they did not make any changes. After you have done so, attempt to sign in to your account.
>
> If you are able to sign in, take the steps outlined below to secure your account.
>
> If you are not able to sign in, contact eBay for additional assistance. If your account has been compromised, eBay will work with you to secure your account. eBay will send you a request that you change your password (not provide your password) and may place a temporary hold on your account.
>
> Educate yourself on how to recognize and report spoof email and Web sites impersonating eBay. The most common way for an eBay account to be compromised is through spoof emails designed to access members' passwords and other sensitive information. Please forward any suspicious or unexpected emails claiming to be from eBay to us at the email address spoof@ebay.com. It's also a good idea to review the Spoof Tutorial and other online security information available from the eBay Security and Resolution Center.
>
> Change the password on your personal email account. If a third party has access to your email account, they may be able to gain access to your eBay account. Therefore, it is important to ensure that your email account is secure. Make sure your email account's password is different from your eBay password. Learn about creating a secure password to help prevent any unauthorized account changes in the future.
>
> Request a new eBay password. After you enter your User ID on this page, you are prompted to answer at least one of a number of questions related to your

account. Once you have answered at least one of the questions provided, an email is sent to you with instructions that allow you to complete your password change.

If you are still unable to change your password, review your contact information be sure that the email address on your account is correct, and check the spam filtering settings on your email account to see if the filter is preventing receipt of email from eBay.

Change the Secret Question and Answer on your eBay account. If you don't have a secret question, you can create one now. Read tips on choosing an effective secret question.

Verify your personal contact information registered on your eBay account and change anything that isn't correct. If your account was compromised, the contact information on your account may have been changed without your permission. In addition, if the contact information on your account has not been updated recently, you may need to update the information on your account.

Search for any active bids or listings that may be unauthorized. You can review active bids and listings from your My eBay page. If you find any active bids or listings that are unauthorized, you may be able to retract the bids and end the listings. If you see unauthorized fees when you review your selling account, please contact eBay to request a credit.

Take steps to protect your identity. Sensitive information submitted to eBay, including credit card and bank account information, is stored on a secure server and cannot be accessed through your eBay account. Although this information cannot be obtained through eBay, you should take steps to protect your identity if you provided information to a spoof Web site or replied to a spoofed email.

Contacting eBay

If you are unable to sign in to your eBay account, or if you require additional assistance, contact us immediately through Live Help.

Important: If you have installed pop-up or ad blockers on your computer, temporarily disable them to use Live Help. Once you have finished your Live Help session, re-enable this software immediately. This will ensure your computer is fully protected from pop-ups, ads and spyware.

If you cannot use Live Help:

Email us to report that you cannot sign in to your account.

Email us after signing in to your account to request additional assistance.

Be sure to include the following information:

- Name and address
- Phone number (with the best time to reach you)
- User ID
- Email address
- Item numbers of any unauthorized transactions
- Brief summary of the situation

Table 6-1

Most institutions will have similar processes in place for regaining access to hi-jacked accounts, as well as a number of recommended procedures for securing them in order to make certain that they do not get hi-jacked again. But make no mistake about it. If you do get your account back without any major damage being done to it, or with it, then you will be one of the very lucky ones. Most people who end up with their accounts being hi-jacked lose a lot more than the time and effort spent in trying to have them restored.

Heed The Warnings

Unlike a variety store that gets robbed at gun-point, or your car which gets taken by some car thief, eBay, PayPal and other accounts do not get stolen. They are most often simply given away by their owners through carelessness on their part.

Most if not all financial and other membership based organizations, including PayPal and eBay, quite frequently warn their members about the receipt of such fake e-mails, and that among other things, they should be ignored. Yet, despite such continual warnings, there are still numerous accounts hi-jacked daily. So while this information is certainly not by any means complete, hopefully it will be enough to make you aware that these things do happen, and help you avoid being victimized by such scams.

NOTE: If you should receive such an e-mail claiming to be from eBay or PayPal, and either determine that it is a fake, or perhaps are in doubt as to whether or not it is authentic, please forward it to either spoof@ebay.com or spoof@paypal.com accordingly. Or in the case of an e-mail claiming to be from some other organization, forward it to the security office of that particular institution.

So if you have read this chapter very carefully, fully understand it, and pay attention to the frequent legitimate e-mails which you receive from those organizations where you have a membership, your account should never be hi-jacked by anyone. In other words, if after reading this chapter, you still reply to some e-mail you receive, or visit some website as directed in the e-mail to do, and provide your personal account information, I feel sorry for you, as unfortunately, you have learned very little.

Chapter 7

Dealing With Customers

The Customer Is Always Right

Regardless of how good or how fair a retailer you may be, or ever hope to be, there will no doubt be times when you will find your view of "the customer is always right" being pushed to the limit, if not beyond it.

It is very probable that you will come across a few customers who will have their very own concept of fairness. In their eyes, the only way to do business will be "their" way. Sadly, they are the ones who, no matter how hard you may try to please them, will likely not see things as most normal people would see them. Only too often, they are also the ones who will make mistakes due to a lack of either knowledge or experience, or perhaps even through some degree of carelessness. But then, rather than accept any degree of responsibility for their own actions, will want to find someone else to blame for their shortcomings, and the situation which they find themselves in.

In such cases, it will more likely than not, be the sellers who will take the brunt of their anger. And then when things do not pan out exactly as they had expected, they will turn against eBay or some other organization for allowing such sellers [you] to even exist in the first place. Heaven knows, I have come across a few of them, and no doubt, as a seller, you will too. But relax! There are many ways to help balance the scales to ensure that you as a retailer are not at such a big disadvantage as you might otherwise be. If you follow the suggestions presented in this book for listing items, disclosing all relative information, dealing with feedback, and so on, I am certain that your overall experience will be much more enjoyable than it might otherwise be.

There are a number of "rules of the road" which every seller should not only be fully aware of, but should always adopt in order not to be taken advantage of by unreasonable customers. Such rules include how items are described, how payments are accepted and processed, how shipping and handling charges are calculated and shown, how and when items are shipped, and last but certainly not least, when it comes to dealing on eBay, how you handle disputes, feedback and non-paying bidders.

Failure to follow such rules will not only lead to many bouts of needless frustration and headaches, but in more extreme cases, will most adversely affect your overall business.

Item & Delivery Disputes

There are essentially 4 types of disputes which buyers can file against you with regards to credit card transactions:

1. Charge Not Authorized
2. Charge Not As Authorized
3. Item Not Received
4. Item Not As Described [Advertised]

If you require all your customers to go through PayPal, you will virtually eliminate the first two of those dispute possibilities. In order to be protected however from disputes 3 and 4, you will need to understand PayPal's rules and how they will apply to you, and your business.

Item Not Received

If and when you have a customer who files an 'Item Not Received' claim against you, you will need to be able to prove that the item was in fact delivered, or that a delivery attempt was made. If you do not, you will be forced to provide a full refund for the item, including all shipping and handling charges that your customer paid you. In order to prove delivery, you will need to provide PayPal with a Delivery Confirmation for the item.

Normally, a Delivery Confirmation is the only proof of delivery which PayPal will accept. If however your Delivery Confirmation shows that the item is at Customs, or at the recipient's local post office waiting to be picked up, even though technically the customer has not yet received it, PayPal will most often accept that as proof of the item being delivered.

Tracking Numbers vs. Delivery Confirmations: The Difference

There is often a vast misunderstanding in the difference between a 'Tracking Number' and a 'Delivery Confirmation'.

A 'Tracking Number' is just that. It is a tracking number which allows monitoring (either online or by telephone) of the progress of a shipment, up to and including its delivery. Contrary to popular opinion, tracking numbers are accepted as Proof of Delivery by PayPal so long as the 'tracking number' shows that the item has been delivered, and the value is $250 US or less. If the item however is valued at more than $250 US, a tracking number alone will not be sufficient, as a signature is also required.

A 'Delivery Confirmation' is also a tracking number of sorts, but without the point-to-point tracking available with tracking numbers. A Delivery Confirmation will show that an item has been delivered, and depending on the options chosen, can also show a signature for the delivery, either online or through hard copy. PayPal accepts Delivery Confirmations as Proof of Delivery, but requires that they also include a signature if the amount is over $250 US.

Item Significantly Not As Described [Advertised]

Regardless of how good a seller you may be, or how accurately you have described your items, there will most likely be times in which you will find customers who will not be happy with their purchases for one reason or another. Some will blame you for misrepresenting the item, even though you may not have done so, while others will simply want refunds because they have changed their minds. Either way, they will likely attempt to re-negotiate the sale after the fact. And should they not succeed, they may file a 'Significantly Not As Described' dispute against you. Now if you think for even the briefest moment, that placing a notice on your auction or website that the 'Sale is Final' or that the item is being sold 'As Is', it is now time to dispel such a notion. In the world of online retailing, such disclaimers mean nothing.

If and when a customer files a 'Significantly Not As Advertised' dispute against you, you will most likely have to provide at least a partial refund. With luck, you will be able to negotiate with your customer just how much of a refund you will need to provide, and whether or not such a refund will require return of the item. Your negotiating success will of course depend largely on why your customer wants a refund in the first place, such as whether he is claiming the item was misrepresented, or that he finds it not suitable for his purpose, or that he is simply changing his mind.

The good news however is that if you are unable to negotiate a satisfactory refund amount, and your customer insists on a full refund, he will need to return the item to you at his expense, and will also need to ship it to you in a manner which will provide Delivery Confirmation acceptable to PayPal.

You will however need to keep in mind, that while PayPal will require your buyer to provide valid tracking information showing that the item was indeed returned to you, you will not be allowed to simply refuse delivery of it, and thus avoid having to give a refund. If the tracking information provided shows that a delivery attempt was made, PayPal will accept that as being just as good as Proof of Delivery, and will refund your buyer. Therefore you need to fully understand, that if you refuse to accept delivery of a returned item, you will not only be giving a refund, but you could also be out the cost of the item if it gets returned to your buyer. If that happens, your buyer will be under no further obligation to pay you for the item, or to return it at any additional expense to him.

Leaving Feedback For Your Buyers

Sellers who normally provide feedback for their buyers as

soon as items are paid for, more than likely will have more negatives than they would otherwise have or perhaps deserve. If this applies to you, it may be a good idea to change such a policy.

Given the rapid growth and popularity of online auctions, such as eBay provides, there are more and more new members coming on board every day. Some of them unfortunately have little or no concept of actual delivery times, or that many things can happen in the shipping process over which sellers will have little if any control. While most buyers know that a letter can often go from one major city to another in just one or two business days, some buyers unreasonably expect that parcels, even to International destinations, will travel at the same rate of speed.

Then of course, there are those buyers who somehow think that sellers are offering an overnight courier service for their items, even though they may be charging a mere $4 to $5 total S&H. Others will often confuse the word "shipped" with the word "delivered", or perhaps complain that they were charged $X for S&H but that there was only $Y postage on the item when it arrived. And since they have no concept of the meaning of the word "handling" as in S&H, they now expect a refund of the difference. Believe me! I have come across a few such buyers. If you leave feedback first, you will be leaving yourself wide open to the whims of such unreasonable people.

The bottom line is that holding off on leaving feedback first will greatly reduce the number of negatives which you might otherwise receive, often through no fault of yours. I have seen a great deal of negative feedback left for sellers in which buyers stated "so and so", such as item not "brand new" as described, or "seller claimed such and such" to be the case, but then upon examination of the auction description, I saw that they were 100% wrong. The auctions clearly stated that the items were "refurbished", "like new", "used 9 months", etc. This comes back to our discussion earlier in this book about some buyers not reading auction descriptions. Some do not! Sellers however, should not have to pay for the mistakes made by such buyers.

Non-Paying Bidders

I also find it to not be in the best interest of sellers to leave negative feedback for non-paying bidders. In most cases, leaving negatives for non-payment accomplishes nothing except an assurance of getting negatives in return from those buyers whose accounts are still active by the time they realize that they received negatives. Filing Unpaid Item Disputes [UIDs] on the other hand is very effective. In fact, nothing is more effective at getting deadbeat buyers to actually pay for the auctions they won, or at helping to rid eBay of those who see the whole process of winning auctions and then not paying for them, as being merely another form of entertainment. From our own experience, I have found that filing UIDs has a 30% chance of getting money owed. And from correspondence with other sellers, it would appear that they have experienced similar results.

Unfortunately, there are far too many eBay sellers who do not follow this way of thinking. They leave negatives for non-payment, but then do not file UIDs as they should. As a result, many non-paying bidders end up with accounts riddled with numerous negatives for non-payment, yet are still able to continue their game of bidding and not paying with seller after seller. Had those sellers filed UIDs as they should have, such non-paying bidders would have been suspended from eBay after only 3 non-payments.

Filing UIDs is also a very effective way of getting reimbursed by those who decided to chargeback their credit cards after they received their items. In such cases, an e-mail or letter sent to them at the same time as you file your claim, reminding them of the act of fraud they are committing, will go a very long way towards helping them see the light.

Non-paying bidders need to be stopped. It is up to every seller to help stop them in much the same way as those who are poor credit risks eventually are no longer able to obtain credit.

Now if you would rather just not have to deal with Non-Paying Bidders at all, there is a way to make that happen (other than of course leaving eBay). Here is a 2-step process to accomplish this:

1. Set up all your auctions in "Fixed Price" format.

2. Require immediate payment for your 'Buy it Now' transactions. Note that this option will require that you accept PayPal as your method of payment, and that your buyers will have to use PayPal in order to pay for their items.

Mutual Feedback Withdrawal

Every eBay member should be fully aware of eBay's Mutual Feedback Withdrawal Option. A similar option was once available exclusively through SquareTrade, but only after paying them a $20 fee to arbitrate the underlying dispute which led to the unfavorable feedback. Unfortunately, SquareTrade's arbitration process was not binding, so as a result, it ended when either side refused to co-operate, and thus no resolution was reached.

In any case, part of the SquareTrade arbitration process was to obtain agreement from both sides in the dispute to have their respective feedback comments removed. At that time, provided both sides agreed, not only were their negative feedback counts adjusted downwards, but the actual comments were removed completely from feedback profiles, with no trace of them left behind. SquareTrade can no longer do this. They can now only adjust downward a member's negative count, but the comments will still remain in the profile with a notation that they have been "mutually" withdrawn. eBay now offers this exact same option directly, and for free.

Nonetheless, adopting a feedback policy as I have described here should reduce the number of negatives or neutrals which you might otherwise receive, perhaps through no fault of yours. But in the event that you do receive a few negatives from unreasonable buyers, you will be in a much better position to negotiate a settlement with your buyers, including an agreement to mutually withdraw any feedback left so as to not affect your overall feedback rating. Some will argue that this approach to feedback simply fosters retaliatory feedback from the other side. Perhaps! But it also encourages both sides to communicate. And with communication, there is most always a resolution found, which is exactly what should have happened in the first place. So label it as you will, but it does work, and as a result, everyone wins!

The Responsibility Rests With You

Remember that while *Drop Shipping* has it many advantages, you as a seller, will be 100% responsible for ensuring that your customers get their products in a timely manner, and that those products are exactly as you advertised them to be. It will not be an acceptable excuse for you to claim that you are not responsible simply because your supplier did not deliver as expected, or as you contracted him to do.

Remember also that it is *your* reputation which is on the line with *your* customers. If your supplier does not deliver as you expect, or as your customers expect, you will have some rather unhappy customers, not to mention, a somewhat less-than-desired reputation. Maintaining a good reputation on eBay is hard enough in itself. Don't let some careless supplier ruin *yours* for you.

While it would be fair to accept the old cliché that "anyone can make a mistake", when it comes to *Drop Shipping*, we really should draw the line on that much sooner than we might otherwise do. After one or two mistakes, we would be wise to seek out a new supplier for such problem items or service, or certainly obtain some reliable assurance that such mistakes will not happen again. Perhaps even a penalty system in place to compensate you in some way if they do happen to screw up again would be an excellent deterrent. I can however tell you this: If you become complacent and accepting of poor service, more likely than not, such complacency will simply foster an even greater decline in service. Sadly, this seems to be a somewhat universal problem in almost any aspect of business. What we tolerate will, more often than not, become the norm.

In any event, it will be up to you, the seller, to make absolutely certain that the items being shipped to your customers are exactly as advertised by both you and your supplier. It would be a very good idea to test this for yourself by soliciting honest feedback from your customers. And I do not mean through eBay's feedback system, but rather through a direct one-on-one communication with your customers. For some of you, that may seem like a rather scary thought I know! How dare I suggest that you ever solicit feedback from your customers on how you performed as a seller? Nonetheless, the bottom line here is to determine if your customers are getting the quality of products and service from your suppliers as you would hope they are getting. There are several ways of determining this without actually letting on that you use a drop shipper to deliver your items. Be creative! Here are two excellent ways to get you started.

1. Arrange to have an item or two shipped to people you know, preferably in another city. That way, you can follow up with them to hopefully get an accurate indication of the quality of the item, how it was packaged, how it was shipped, when it was shipped, the amount actually paid for shipping versus the amount you were charged by your drop shipper, and of course, how long it took to reach them.

2. Contact a few of your customers and tell them you are following up on their orders to make sure that everything was OK. They will appreciate that perhaps more than you realize. You might tell them something to the effect that you have just changed shipping companies because the last one you dealt with did not adequately package your items. And of course, you now want to make sure that your new company does a much better job. You will most always get a reply to the effect that "Everything was great!" or "It was OK, BUT...".

It is the "BUT" that you should be particularly concerned with. It is the "BUT" that will tell you that something did not go quite as your customer had expected, or as you had expected. Either way, respond promptly to their input. Be sure and thank them for their input, and of course correct any problems if there are any. And perhaps even provide them with some kind of a coupon to be used against a future purchase. Your customers will love you for it. Guaranteed!

In short, you are the seller! So when (not if) problems arise, it will be you and you alone who must fix them, or have them fixed. And remember that while much of this simply makes good business sense, dealing on eBay is much different than dealing through your own website, or through your own 'bricks & mortar' retail store. With either of the latter, you have the ability to set your own policies, and then either follow or ignore them as you see fit. But when dealing on eBay, and/or using PayPal as a payment method, both eBay and PayPal will add their own sets of policies to the pot. It is those policies which you must adhere to, even if some of them may perhaps vary from your own policies, and your way of doing business.

Many suspended sellers from eBay unfortunately had a much different take on this. Thus they had to learn the hard way.

Neither eBay nor PayPal will tolerate sellers who receive many complaints for non-delivery of items. Nor will they tolerate sellers, who receive many complaints for items not being as advertised, or for items which were received defective in one way or another, but yet made no effort to resolve such problems with their buyers.

Of course most, including eBay and PayPal, acknowledge and accept the fact that there will always be a small number of such complaints. It is simply par for the course in any business. Problems however do occur for any of a number of reasons, and not necessarily through any fault of sellers. Problems sometimes occur due to a lack of communication between buyer and seller. Problems however do escalate as a result of sellers making little or no attempt to deal with issues as they are brought to their attention. This is where good customer service comes in, and plays its most important part. When problems do arise, you as a seller must solve them no matter what it takes, within reason of course. No one will fault you if you do all you reasonably can to resolve a problem, but your customer remains quite irrational about the whole situation. It happens! Learn to deal with it and then move on.

The crucial point to remember is that regardless of the origin of problems, if you are not responsive to your buyers' concerns, complaints will likely be filed against *you*. Once this happens, a trend of *bad* business practice will be quickly established, the damage from which will be very difficult, if not impossible, to undo.

eBay is a wonderful place to do business, and using *Drop Shipping* to supply products to your customers can be a very lucrative way of conducting that business. All you need do is fully understand the rules, and work within their parameters. And above all...never lose sight of the *Golden Rule*: "Do unto others as you would have them do unto you." In other words, never treat someone else in a way that you would not like to be treated. The rest should be easy!

Afterword

While no book can realistically cover every imaginable scenario which could occur in this business, it is my hope that this one has provided you with most of the tools necessary to help you avoid the many pitfalls which the uninformed merchant might otherwise encounter. It is also my hope that you have discovered what you need to look for when considering any company with which to deal, and that you now know how to select and sell your products in a manner which will provide you with the best possible outcome. Over time, you will no doubt discover what works best for you.

The multitudes of products offered in our **Drop Shipping For GOLD** Directory should be more than adequate to either get you started in a brand new business, or help you to expand an existing one. To add to any product line will not be difficult once your have set your goals, and know exactly what it is you wish to accomplish. And if you still want more products, I would certainly recommend any of the fine directories and resources listed below. They should provide you with more than a lifetime worth of products. See Special Offer on page 115 of this book. Website: http://www.dropshippingforgold.com/

Canadian Trade Index - The Canadian Trade Index provides detailed information regarding over 32,000 Canadian companies, including 30,000 Manufacturers, 11,500 Active Exporters, 7,000 Distributors of products in Canada, and 3,700 Service companies for manufactured products. FREE. Website: http://www.ctidirectory.com/

Hoover's Industry Directory - Insightful information about industries, companies, and the people who lead them. All packages include access to Hoover's Global Powerhouse of

public, non-public, and international companies, as well as industries and key people. Contact information and vital statistics are included for all companies within a specific region (US/Canada, UK, Europe, Asia/Pacific). FREE Trial.
Website: http://www.hoovers.com/free/industries/

Scottsinfo.com - A membership based web site containing the Scott's Directories Corporate database of Canadian Manufacturers, Wholesalers, Distributors, Industrial and B2B Services, and much more. A 14-Day FREE Trial.
Website: http://www.scottsinfo.com/

Also, any **Chamber of Commerce** (US / Canadian) will be able to provide you with extensive information on a variety of companies and product sources within their respective areas.
Website (USA): http://www.uschamber.com/
Website (Canada): http://www.chamber.ca/

And finally, regardless of what items you may wish to sell, or how you may wish to sell them, be it on eBay or elsewhere, make certain that you read and fully understand all the policies which apply to your chosen site. This will ensure that your time there will be as enjoyable and as rewarding as possible. And once again, always try and live by the Golden Rule, whether you are dealing with a Customer, or with a Supplier. When you do, you will likely find that no problem will be insurmountable.

So until we meet again...Good Luck, and may God Bless!

Glossary

Authorized Distributor - A distributor which has been authorized by a manufacturer to offer its products for sale to either wholesalers or retailers

Authorized Retailer - A retailer which has been authorized by either a manufacturer, a distributor, or a wholesaler to offer its products for sale to consumers

B&M Store - Bricks & Mortar Store - The eCommerce terms used to refer to a typical off-line store such as a retail establishment in a mall, etc.

BIN - Buy It Now - An eBay auction listing option which gives a potential buyer the opportunity to immediately purchase an item for a pre-specified amount rather than go through the normal bidding process

Chargeback - A dispute filed by a credit card holder claiming that he did not authorize the charge, that the charge was not in the amount that he authorized, that he did not receive the item he paid for, or that the item was not as advertised

Confirmed Shipping Address - An address which has been reviewed and confirmed by PayPal to be a valid address of the PayPal member

Contract - An agreement made between a buyer and a seller to complete a transaction according to certain pre-determined terms and conditions

Copyright - A protection granted to, or acquired by, an author or author-designated party, of certain original material created by that author; Copyright applies to all original literary, dramatic, musical and artistic works

Copyright Violation - The use of any copyrighted material without the permission of the copyright holder; also see Copyright

DC - Delivery Confirmation - A confirmation received by the shipper of an item by either e-mail, website, or hard-copy showing the actually delivery of an item to the intended address; may also include a signature of the recipient, and is usually accompanied by a tracking number; also see Tracking Number

Demand Draft - A check without the account holder's signature on it, and issued by a third party under the claimed authority of the account holder for the purpose of charging the account holder's bank account; may contain the account holder's name or account number; a notation that the customer authorized the draft; and a statement such as "No signature required", "Authorization on file", "Signature on file", etc.; also see Unauthorized Demand Draft

Distributor - A Middleman between a Manufacturer and its Wholesalers; a Distributor may represent many Manufacturers and sell to many Wholesalers; also see Wholesaler

DRM - Digital Rights Management - A security system designed for the protection of copyright interests associated with the distribution of downloadable digital media

Drop Shipper - A company which will sell products to you, and then ship the items directly to your customers on your behalf

Dutch Auction - An auction-type listing which offers multiple, identical items for sale, but unlike a regular auction, can have many winners

eBay - The world's leading member-based online marketplace for the sale of goods and services by a diverse International community of businesses and individuals

eCommerce - The process of conducting business over the Internet; the process of buying and selling goods and services online

E-Mail Header - The identifying text at the beginning of an e-mail message which is generated by both the e-mail client program that first sends it and the mail servers which the e-mail's passes through on route to its final destination; Each node adds more text to the header, including from/to addresses, subject, content type, time stamp and other identification data

Exporting - The process of selling products to customers in another country, and having them shipped to that country from your own

Fake - Not authentic; not original; not authorized; also see Knock-Off; also see VeRO

Feedback - Comments left for buyers or sellers intended to reflect the level of satisfaction experienced with a particular transaction

Fixed Price Listing - An eBay listing option which does not allow bidding, but rather requires a potential buyer to immediately purchase an item for the specified amount

Fraud – The intentional misrepresentation or concealment of information for the purpose of deceiving or misleading; also see Misrepresentation

FVF - Final Value Fee - The fee (commission) which eBay charges sellers upon the successful sale of an item

Grey Market - A source of products not authorized by the product's manufacturer; a source in violation of the manufacturer's distribution agreement

GST - Goods and Services Tax - A Canadian Federal Value Added Tax; charged on most sales at all levels of distribution; tax is a fixed rate for all Canadians; must possess a GST license in order to charge this tax; also see VAT (Value Added Tax)

Identity Theft - The process of acquiring someone else's identity for the purpose of impersonating that person for financial gain, either by stealing from him, or by using his established reputation; also see Phishing

Importing - The process of purchasing products from a supplier in another country and having those products delivered to your own

Inventory - Items manufactured or purchased and held in stock ready for sale

Knock-Off - A product manufactured without the permission of the original patent/trademark/copyright holder; also see Fake

License - Permission granted by one party to another as part of an agreement between the two parties; also see Licensor; also see Licensee

Licensee - The party to whom the license has been granted; also see License; also see Licensor

Licensor - The party granting the License; also see License; also see Licensee

Liquidation - The final-sale of products at any level of the distribution chain; such products may include bankrupt stock, overstocks, store returns, refurbished items, as well as manufacturer's seconds, clearances, and discontinued items; also see Liquidator

Liquidator - A company which acquires products from any of a number of sources, for the purpose of selling those products on a final-sale basis to buyers at any level of the distribution chain; also see Liquidation

Listing Fees - The basic and optional fees which eBay charges sellers to list their items; also see FVF (Final Value Fees)

Misrepresentation - A statement made by a party to a contract that something is fact when in fact, it is not; also see Fraud

MO - Modus Operandi - Mode of Operation; behavior patterns that indicate specific types of fraud; method of operating or functioning; someone's habits or manner of working

MSRP - Manufacturer's Suggested Retail Price - A price estimated by a product's manufacturer to be the intended retail selling price of the item before any wholesale or retail discounts are applied

NIB - New In Box - A commonly used term describing an eBay item's condition

NR - No Reserve - A commonly used term describing an eBay listing which has no reserve bid on the item; item will be sold to the highest bidder

NWOT - New Without Tags - Term used to describe brand new merchandise which have had the manufacturer's original tags removed

NWT - New With Tags - Term used to describe brand new merchandise which still have the manufacturer's original tags attached

Paradigm - A set of assumptions, concepts, values, and practices that constitutes a way of viewing reality for the community that shares them

Patent - A protection granted to, or acquired by, a company or an individual covering new inventions (process, machine, manufacture, composition of matter), or any new and useful improvement of an existing invention

Patent Infringement - Use of a patented design or process without the permission of the patent holder; also see Patent

PayPal - A member-based system that lets anyone with an email address securely send and receive online payments using their credit card and/or bank account

Phishing - The process of sending an e-mail to someone falsely claiming to be from an established legitimate organization, the sole purpose of which is to mislead the recipient into providing their private information which will be used for identity theft purposes; also see Spoof E-Mail; also see Spoof Website; also see Identity Theft

PST - Provincial Sale Tax - A Canadian Provincial Sales Tax; normally charged to the end user (consumer) only; tax rate varies by province; must possess a PST license in order to charge this tax

Reserved Price - An eBay auction listing option which gives a seller an opportunity to select and hide a minimum amount at which he is willing to sell his item, with no obligation to sell the item if bids do not reaches that amount

Retailer - A company which sells directly to the end user or consumer; depending on a manufacturer's distribution flow, retailers may purchase products directly from the manufacturer, or from any of its distributors or wholesalers

RMA - Return Merchandise Authorization - The authorization given by a merchant to a customer to return an item for refund, replacement, or repair; also see RMA Number

RMA Number - The number provided by a merchant to a customer as part of the RMA process, which usually must be attached to the item being returned; also see RMA

Seller Non-Performance - A dispute filed with eBay against a seller who either does not deliver the product sold, or else delivers a product which is substantially different from the one advertised

Spoof E-Mail - An e-mail which is sent as part of a phishing process; also see Phishing

Spoof Website - A fake website designed to appear to be that of an established legitimate organization, but solely for phishing purposes; also see Phishing

Tracking Number - A number provided by a postal or courier service to enable online verification of a shipment's progress and/or its delivery; usually part of the delivery confirmation process; also see Delivery Confirmation

Trademark - A protection granted to, or acquired by, a company or an individual covering words, symbols, designs (or a combination of these), used to distinguish the goods and services of one person or organization from those of others in the marketplace

Trademark Violation - Use of a trademark without permission or acknowledgement of the trademark's owner or agent; also see Trademark

UID - Unpaid Item Dispute - A dispute filed with eBay against a buyer (bidder) who successfully won an auction, or used the 'Buy It Now' option to purchase an item, but did not pay for it; part of the eBay's Unpaid Item Process

Unauthorized Demand Draft - A Demand Draft that the account holder did not authorize to be initiated; also see Demand Draft

Value For Duty - Normally the total amount paid by the customer for the item including any shipping and handling charges paid

VAT - Value Added Tax - A consumption tax which is levied at each stage of production based on the value added to the product at that stage; also see GST (Goods and Services Tax)

Verified PayPal Account - A PayPal account which either has a bank account added and confirmed, or has been approved for a PayPal Plus Credit Card

VeRO - Verified Rights Owner - The owner of intellectual property, such as patents, trademarks, and copyrights; also see Copyright; also see Patent; also see Trademark

Wholesale Price - The price at which products are sold by wholesalers to retailers

Wholesaler - A middleman between a manufacturer or distributor and a Retailer; a wholesaler may represent many manufacturers or distributors; also see Distributor

Special Offer

SPECIAL OFFER! As a Customer of our Drop Shipping For Sellers Book (this Book), for a limited time only, you can get **$10.00 OFF** the regular $24.95 price of our Drop Shipping For Gold eBook and 2007 Drop Shipper Directory, featuring more than 1 million products from 55 of North America's best Drop Shippers. But you must use the **Special Offer** order link below. The price will be adjusted automatically to **ONLY $14.95** at checkout to reflect your **$10.00 discount**. Your Unlock Code will be sent to you by e-mail following payment. So please make sure that the e-mail address you provide when you order is accurate.

For more information on our eBook/Directory, please visit our website at http://www.DropShippingForGold.com, however please keep in mind that you will need to order it through the link below in order to receive your **$10.00 discount**.

Special Offer Link:

    http://www.dropshippingforgold.com/special.html

NOTES

NOTES

NOTES